Eben-Emael

Eben-Emael

IAN KEMP

Ian Allan
PUBLISHING

Acknowledgements:
The author wishes to thank the following:
John Prigent and Thomas Anderson for assitance in locating images. Guy Bastiaens and Yves Haepers at Fort Eben-Emael. Chris Foss for reference material. Terry Gander for photographs of the weaponry. Philip Jarrett for illustrations of the DFS 230 and other aircraft from his extensive archive. David Fletcher, historian at the Tank Museum, Bovington.

Bibliography/sources
Terry Gander, *The Explosive Attack on Fort Eben-Emael.* Fort, Volume Sixteen, 1988.
Joseph W. A. Whitehorne, *The Liege Forts and Eben Emael.* Fort, Volume 32, 2004.
T. N. Mouat, *A New Method of Attack, The German Assault on Eben-Emael, 10 May 1940.* Osprey Military Journal, Volume 2, Issue 3, 2000.
J. E. Kaufmann and R. M. Jurga, *Fortress Europe.* Greenhill Books, 1999.
Henri Lecluse, *Ceux du Fort d'Eben-Emael.* Amicale du Fort d'Eben-Emael.
Special Operations: Case Studies in Special Operations Warfare – Theory and Practice, Presidio Press, 1990.
James Mrazek, *The Fall of Eben Emael.* Presidio Press, 1970.
Napier Crookenden, *Airborne at War.* Ian Allan, 1978.
It Happened Here: Fort Eben-Emael. After the Battle, Number 5, 1974.
William Fowler, *France, Holland and Belgium 1940-1941.* Ian Allan, 2002.
Chris Ellis, *7th Flieger Division.* Ian Allan, 2002.
Bruce Quarrie, *German Airborne Troops 1939-45.* Osprey, 1983.

Bruce Quarrie, *German Airborne Divisions Blitkreig 1940-41.* Osprey, 2004.
James Lucas, *Storming Eagles.* Arms & Armour, 1988.
Rene Vliegen, *Fort Eben-Emael.* Association pour l'etude, la conservation et la protection du fort d'Eben-Emael et de son site, 1993.
Gerard M. Devlin, *Silent Wings, The Story of the Glider Pilots of World War II.* W. H. Allen, 1985.
Christopher Ailsby, *Hitler's Sky Warriors German Paratroopers in Action, 1939-1945.* Brassey's, 2000.
Chris Mcnab, *German Paratroopers of World War II.* Motorbooks International, 2000.
Alan Wood, *History of the World's Glider Forces.* Patrick Stephens, 1990.
Bruce Quarrie, *Airborne assault: parachute forces in action, 1940-1991.* Patrick Stephens, 1991.
Bruce Quarrie, *Fallschirmjäger German Paratrooper 1939-45.* Osprey, 2001.
Jean Paul Pallud, *Blitzkrieg in the West Then and Now.* After the Battle, 1991.
James Lucas, *Kommando: German Special Forces of World War Two.* Arms and Armour Press, 1985.
Thomas B. Gukeisen, *The Fall of Fort Eben Emael: The Effects of Emerging Technologies on the Successful Completion of Military Operations.* US Army Command and General Staff College, 2004.
Rudolf Witzig, *Coup from the air: the capture of Fort Eben-Emael.* History of the Second World War, 1966.
Peter C. Smith, *Dive bomber! An Illustrated History.* Naval Institute Press, 1982.
J. R. Smith and Anthony L. Kay, *German Aircraft of the Second World War.* Putnam 1978.
Bernard Vanden Bloock, *Belgian Fortifications, May 1940.* World War II Online – Technical Publications, 2005.

Series Created & Edited by Jasper Spencer-Smith.
Design and artwork: Nigel Pell.
Cover design: Crispin Goodall.
Cartography: Martin Watts.
Four-colour scanning: Bournemouth Digital Press.
Produced by JSS Publishing Limited,
PO. Box 6031, Bournemouth, Dorset, England.

First published 2006

ISBN (10) 0 7110 3092 8
ISBN (13) 978 0 7110 3092 3

Published by Ian Allan Publishing

an imprint of Ian Allan Publishing Ltd,
Hersham, Surrey KT12 4RG.
Printed by Ian Allan Printing Ltd,
Hersham, Surrey KT12 4RG.

Code: 0604/xx

Visit the Ian Allan Publishing website at:
www.ianallanpublishing.com

CONTENTS

On 10 May 1940, German forces attacked Belgium, Holland and France in what was to become known as Blitzkrieg (lightning war).

1

FALL GELB

The original German plan, codenamed *Fall Gelb* (Case Yellow), developed by the *Oberkommando der Wehrmacht* (OKW – High Command of the Armed Forces) for the invasion of Belgium, Holland and France, was essentially an updated version of the Schlieffen Plan. The *Schwerpunkt* ('point of the spear' or main effort) would be through the Maastricht Appendix in an effort to outflank the Maginot Line and draw the Anglo-French armies into a decisive battle in northern Belgium. The innovative use of tanks, close air support and airborne forces would compensate for the lack of originality. An alternative was developed by *Generalmajor* Erich von Manstein, Chief of Staff of General Karl von Rundstedt's Army Group A, and corps commander General Heinz Guderian. This shifted the *Schwerpunkt* south against Sedan on the River Meuse. Because the region bordered Belgium it was not heavily protected and Manstein believed that German forces would be able to smash through and drive rapidly through northern France to the Channel. This plan was referred to as a *Sichelschnitt* (sickle cut). To achieve surprise three Panzer corps would approach the

Left: **A PzKpfw III Ausf D of the 7th Panzer Division engages an anti-tank gun during the invasion of France. The location is Château Quesnoy, Airaines, near Amiens, 6 June 1940.** *(TM)*

Above: **A stick of** *Fallschirmjäger* **(paratroops) drop from a Junkers Ju52 transport. These troops were used to great effect in the attack on Holland.** *(JSS)*

French border through the wooded and mountainous terrain of the Belgian Ardennes. French planners believed that if the region was properly defended it would be impenetrable to tanks.

On 10 January 1940 the Belgian authorities obtained a copy of the operational order for *Luftflotte* (the original OKW plan) when a *Luftwaffe* liaison aircraft inadvertently landed in Belgium because of bad weather. A furious Hitler endorsed the *Sichelschnitt* plan. It was realised that the security breach could work to Germany's advantage if the British and French could be convinced that the *Schwerpunkt* was still through Maastricht.

Revised orders were issued in February 1940. On the German right *Generaloberst* Fedor von Bock's Army Group B with 29 divisions, including three Panzer divisions, would smash through Belgium and Holland. The two divisions of the *Luftlandekorps* would attack 'Fortress Holland'. *General* Walther von Reichenau's Sixth Army, led by two Panzer divisions, would drive across the Maastricht Appendix as rapidly as possible to link up with *Sturmabteilung Koch*. In the centre Rundstedt's Army Group A with 45 divisions,

Right: **Anti-tank defences silenced, PzKpfw IIIs of the 7th Panzer Division break through the boundary walls of Château Quesnoy.** *(TM)*

Left: **The Junkers Ju87 *Sturzkampf-flugzeug* (Stuka) dive-bomber used for close-support attack for ground forces during *Fall Gelb* (Plan Yellow) in May 1940.** *(JSS)*

including seven Panzer divisions, would move through the Ardennes, force the crossings of the Meuse and then drive to the Channel to cut the Allied armies in half. On the left only the 19 divisions of General Wilhelm von Leeb's Army Group C would be used to mask the Maginot Line.

The *Luftwaffe* was assigned the missions of destroying the Belgian and Dutch air forces on the ground, neutralising the British and French air forces and providing close support for a rapid ground advance.

When Hitler conceived the seizure of Fort Eben-Emael in October 1939 it was intended to secure the route for the German main effort. By May 1940 the operation had become part of a huge deception plan to lure the Anglo-French armies into Belgium and clear an axis of advance through Sedan. For the plan to succeed it was vital that Eben-Emael be silenced and the bridges across the Albert Canal be secured intact as rapidly as possible.

Below: **A German armoured column comprising a PzKpfw Ausf B *Befehlswagen* and two PzKpfw IIIs at a rest stop during the *Blitzkrieg* of May 1940.** *(TA)*

Above: **A PzKpfw I** *Munitionsschlepper* **(munitions carrier) on an Ausf A chassis. The vehicle is passing through ranks of captured Dutch troops, 1940.** *(TAn)*

Right: **A PzKpfw III Ausf E,** *Befehlswagen* **(command tank) moves through a heavily damaged village during the** *Blitzkrieg* **of 1940.** *(TM)*

In 1939, the Belgian Defence Minister promised that the fort would be 'able to withstand the pounding of the heaviest artillery'

2

FORT EBEN-EMAEL

After France's humiliating defeat during the 1870-71 Franco-Prussian War the Belgian government decided that it was only a matter of time before these two great powers would again be at war and that neither would respect Belgium's neutrality. Over the following 20 years Belgium built a series of forts designed by Belgian Army engineer General Henri Brialmont to protect Liège, astride the invasion route from Germany, Namur, which guarded the route from France, and, the vital seaport of Antwerp.

To defend Liège six large forts and six smaller fortins were positioned in a circle about 8km (5 miles) from the city's centre; the interval between each fort was about 3km (1.86 miles). Built between 1888 and 1891 each fort mounted from five to eight artillery pieces, usually 120mm, 150mm and 210mm weapons, in revolving domes. In 1887 General Brialmont recommended building an additional fort in the 'gap of Vise', north of Liège near the village of Eben-Emael. When this was rejected Brialmont predicted that Belgium would 'weep tears of blood because of not having built this fort'. His words proved prophetic when on 4 August 1914 Germany launched the *Fall Schlieffen* to invade northern France through

Left: **Coupole Nord** was raised for the first time in 60 years on 25 November 2000. The lifting gear is hand-operated using cables on a winding drum. *(FE-E)*

Right: **Observation *Coupole Eben I* overlooking the Albert Canal and the Vise Gap.** *(FE-E)*

Right: **Observation *Coupole Eben I* overlooking the Albert Canal and the Vise Gap.** *(FE-E)*

Belgium. The German First Army crossed the Meuse River less than 5km (3.1 miles) south of Eben-Emael.

The Brialmont forts were believed to be among the strongest in Europe but this confidence was soon shown to be unfounded. The use of poor quality unreinforced concrete proved a fatal flaw especially as the thickness – 1.5m (1.92ft) and a 2.5m (8.2ft) layer of sand and stone – was no longer adequate to withstand the heavier weapons in service by 1914. Brialmont's decision to concentrate the heaviest gun cupolas in a central citadel made the forts an easy target

for German fire. To smash the Brialmont forts Germany had developed the Krupp 420mm *Dicke Bertha* ('Big Bertha') howitzer, however the first of the Liège forts fell on 8 August and another on 11 August even before these heavy guns were brought into action. On 12 August two 420mm howitzers and two 305mm Skoda howitzers joined the bombardment and over five days the remaining forts were systematically destroyed. A 420mm shell smashed into the central citadel of Fort Loncin on 15 August and detonated in an ammunition magazine; the resultant explosion shattered the fort. In a similar

Right: **Coupole *Nord* mounted two 75mm FRC Model 1934 guns and a machine gun. The emplacement was attacked by *8 Trupp*.** *(FE-E)*

manner the Germans reduced the forts of Namur and Antwerp.

After the armistice Belgium abandoned its prewar neutrality and on 7 September 1920 signed a defensive pact with France. In March 1920 the French government launched the first of a series of studies on territorial defence that eventually culminated in the 1930s with construction of the Maginot Line from the Swiss border to the supposedly impenetrable Ardennes Forest. Senior Belgian defence officials were divided, with some advocating a strong defence along the eastern border while others favoured a strong defence along the Dyle River. Early in 1929 approval was given to modernise eight of the original 12 Brialmont forts protecting Liège and work was largely completed by 1932. However, it was realised that more credible defences would have to be built if Germany was not to consider an advance through Belgium as an easy option to outflank the Maginot Line. In December 1930 a special defence commission recommended building a defensive line behind the Meuse River and the new 130km (80.7 mile) long Albert Canal that linked Liège

with Antwerp. Besides being an economic boost the government intended the canal to be a formidable barrier to a German invasion. Work on the canal began in 1930 and was completed in 1939.

On 21 April 1931 the government approved a new national defence plan. The improved Brialmont forts were designated the Position Fortifiée de Liège II (PFL II) and construction was approved of a modern series of forts, PFL I, in a 45km (28-mile) long arc to the east of Liège and closer to the border with Germany. PFL I was originally intended to comprise major forts at Eben-Emael, Aubin-Neufchâteau, Battice, Remou-champs and Tancremont with two smaller forts at Comblai-du-Pont and Les Wades. However, the plan to build the two latter forts was dropped at an early stage as an economy measure and construction of Remouchamps had not yet been funded when Germany invaded Poland on 1 September 1939.

Defence Minister Albert Divèze promised that Fort Eben-Emael would be 'able to withstand the pounding of the heaviest artillery'. The fort's precise location was chosen to take maximum advantage of the protection offered by the Albert

*Above: **Bloc V** protected by anti-tank defences. Above the emplacement is **Coupole Sud** which mounted two 75mm guns. In the background along the anti-tank ditch is **Bloc IV**. The photograph is dated May 1940. (JSS)*

bridge was prepared for demolition and if this failed artillery fire from Eben-Emael would destroy the bridges.

Under the supervision of engineer Colonel Jean Mercier the Belgian company Entreprises Réunies began construction of Eben-Emael on 1 April 1932 and the fort was largely completed in 1935 although some minor work was still underway when the fort fell to the Germans in 1940. Eben-Emael was designed in the rough shape of a diamond with the tip pointing north. It measured 900m (2,953ft) from north to south and 800m (2,625ft) at its widest point from east to west and covered an area of 66 hectares (163 acres), much of it on the relatively flat plateau atop St Peter's Mount. The north-eastern flank was protected by the Caster cutting and the northwestern flank by a water-filled anti-tank ditch than ran half the length of the wall. The Geer River that ran into the canal below the fort further protected the north-western flank; this could be dammed to create an inundated floodplain. The southern flanks of the fort were formed by four shorter walls protected by a dry 10m wide, 4m (13.1ft) deep anti-tank ditch. Barbed wire entanglements and anti-tank obstacles covered the approaches to the fort.

Despite its size there was little evidence of Eben-Emael on the surface as the fort was built by tunnelling into the limestone of St Peter's Mount. The only entrance was from the Geer valley through *Bloc 1* into the lowest level about 60m (197ft) below the upper level or superstructure. A wooden bridge in *Bloc 1* could be retracted to create a 4m (13.1ft) deep obstacle. The lowest level contained accommodation for 1,440 troops and six electricity generators, water pumps, kitchens, washrooms and an infirmary to make the garrison entirely self-sufficient. One lift for ammunition and two stairways for personnel provided access from the lower to the intermediate level. The intermediate level, about 45m (147.6ft) below the superstructure, comprised a series of tunnels and galleries running for 4km (2.49 miles) connecting the fighting positions on the superstructure. To avoid a repetition of the disastrous explosion in Fort Loncin's central magazine in 1914 the ammunition in Eben-Emael was dispersed in individual magazines beneath each fighting position. Opposite each ammunition magazine was a shaft for two ammunition lifts and a staircase of 100 to 120 stairs leading to a casemate or cupola

Canal. The canal was linked to the Meuse River by cutting a 1,300m (4.265ft) long channel, known as the Caster cutting, through St Peter's Mount thus effectively creating a moat with almost perpendicular walls about 40m (131ft) high. St Peter's Mount overlooks the Maastricht Appendix, a finger-like projection that points south from Holland to separate Belgium from Germany. The appendix is only 24km (14.9 miles) across at its widest point and the best that Belgian defence planners hoped was that Dutch forces would impose a short delay on German invaders by destroying the bridges across the Maas (Meuse) in the city of Maastricht. With the construction of the Albert Canal the routes from Maastricht into Belgium crossed new bridges at Veldwezelt in the north, Vroenhoven in the centre and Kanne to the south. At times of tension each bridge would be defended by an infantry company sited in concrete pillboxes and other prepared positions and supported by artillery fire from Fort Eben-Emael. Kanne bridge was only 1.6km (0.99 mile) north of the fort, Vroenhofen, 3.2km, (1.99 miles) away and Veldwezelt bridge, 7km, (4.35 miles). Each

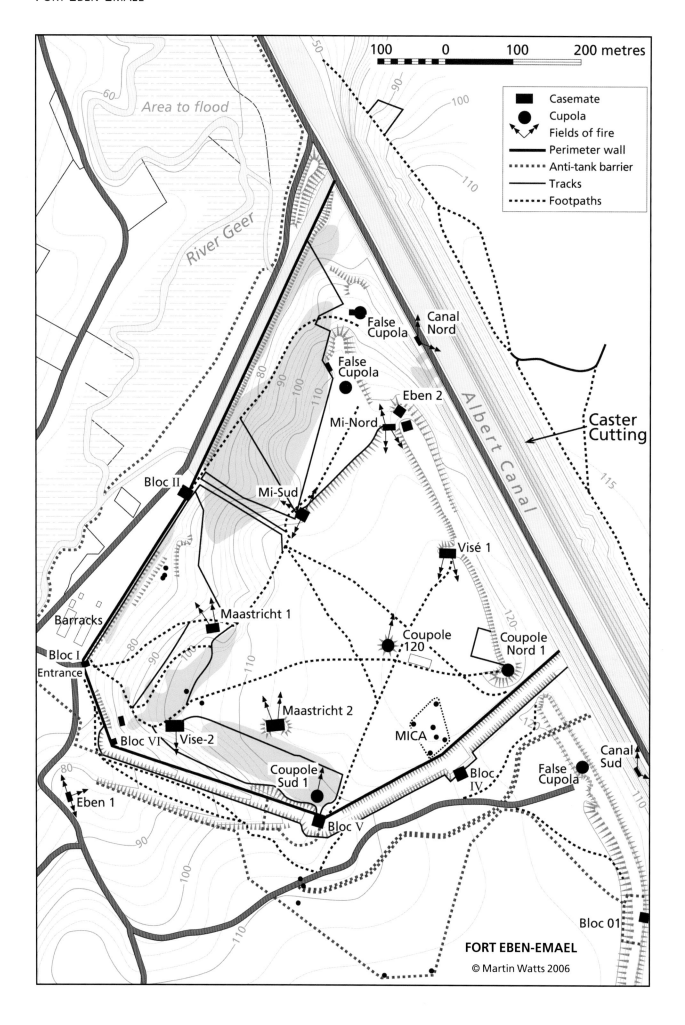

FORT EBEN-EMAEL

© Martin Watts 2006

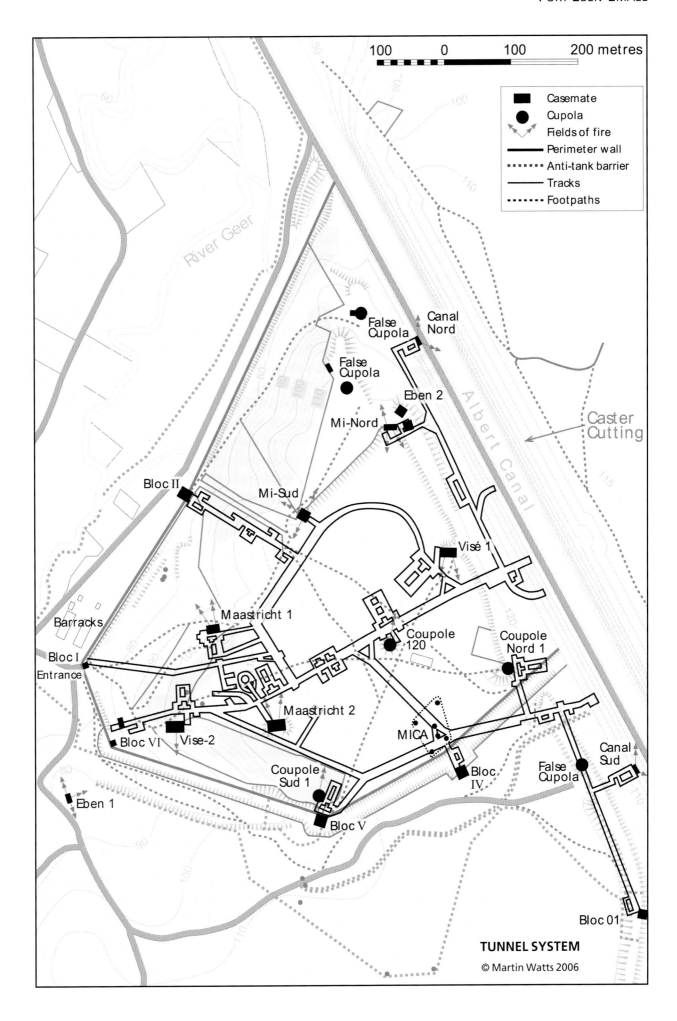

Casemate
Cupola
Fields of fire
Perimeter wall
Anti-tank barrier
Tracks
Footpaths

100   0   100   200 metres

River Geer

False Cupola
Canal Nord
False Cupola
Eben 2
Mi-Nord
Mi-Sud
Bloc II
Visé 1
Albert Canal
Caster Cutting

Barracks
Maastricht 1
Coupole 120
Coupole Nord 1
Bloc I
Entrance
Maastricht 2
MICA
Bloc IV
Canal Sud
False Cupola
Bloc VI
Vise-2
Coupole Sud 1
Eben 1
Bloc V
Bloc 01

TUNNEL SYSTEM

© Martin Watts 2006

15

Left: **Eben 3 observation cupola.** *(JSS)*

on the superstructure. If an enemy gained entry to any of the fighting positions these could be sealed off at the intermediate level by a set of double doors with the interval between the doors blocked using pre-positioned steel beams and sandbags.

The fort's superstructure boasted 17 cupolas, casemates and machine gun bunkers (known as blocs) divided into an offensive battery (*1er Batterie*) and a defensive battery (*2e Batterie*). The heaviest weapons of the *1er Batterie* were two 120mm FRC Model 1931 guns housed in the revolving *Coupole 120* approximately in the fort's centre. These had a maximum range of 18,000m (11.18 miles). Not wanting to provoke Berlin the Belgian government had denied military planners permission to install heavier weapons that could fire into German territory.

Two other armoured turrets, *Coupole Nord* (Cupola North) and *Coupole Sud* (Cupola South), each mounted a pair of 75mm FRC Model 1934 guns with a maximum range of 11,000m (6.84 miles). Unlike the larger, heavier *Coupole 120* these two cupolas could be retracted to reduce their exposure to enemy fire. The three cupolas could be rotated 360^0 to engage targets in any direction. The offensive battery also included four casemates each mounting three 75mm guns that could fire over a 70^0 arc. Two casemates, *Maastricht 1* and *Maastricht 2*, covered targets to the north including the bridges crossing the Albert Canal while casemates *Visé 1* and *Visé 2* covered the south.

The *2e Batterie* comprised the fort's defence bunkers. On the superstructure were two machine

gun bunkers each armed with three 7.65mm Maxim machine guns. There were five bunkers armed with 60mm anti-tank guns and machine guns sited at the angles of the walls to cover the approaches to the fort and the anti-tank ditch. The anti-tank guns had a range of 3km (1.86 miles). Another two bunkers were sited at the bottom of the Caster cut to prevent any attempt to cross the canal. The defensive battery also included *Bloc 01* that was situated outside the fort to the south to protect the Lanaye locks and observe along the Meuse valley into Holland; it was connected to the fort by a tunnel. Three of the emplacements on the superstructure also incorporated separate observation cupolas.

Although the northern part of the fort was partially covered by woods Eben-Emael was easily identified from the air as it was framed by the Albert Canal to the northeast, the wet moat to the northwest and farmers' fields to the south. German reconnaissance photographs taken secretly by scheduled Lufthansa aircraft clearly identified all of the fort's main features including three dummy cupolas that were built to resemble *Coupole 120*. This deception measure proved effective as German intelligence analysts failed to identify these cupolas as false and they were attacked on 10 May 1940. To defend against air attack an anti-aircraft battery equipped with four *Mitrailleuse Contre Avions* (MICA) machine guns was situated in open pits about 25m (82ft) apart on the superstructure near *Bloc IV*. Between the MICA battery and *Coupole 120*

Right: **Main entrance to Fort Eben-Emael. In the background are the ruins of the barracks.** *(F E-E)*

was a wooden building, called the *Baraque Graindorge*, that was used as a workshop by employees of the *Fonderie Royale de Canons* (FRC) who maintained the fort's heavy weapons.

The commander of Eben-Emael was responsible for two bunkers outside the fort, *Bloc 0* sited to defend the Kanne bridge and *Bloc PL 19* at Hallembaye sited to defend the approach from the Visé bridge. These bunkers were among the 162 built along with anti-tank ditches and other obstacles to cover the intervals between the PFL I forts. These prepared positions were manned by field army units upon mobilisation. The fort's commander was also responsible for six observation posts outside the fort that were connected by telephone line: Loen, Caster 1, Caster 2, Kanne, Vroenhoven and Briegden.

Located on the intermediate level was the fort's command post, telephone exchange, radio room and three fire direction centres (FDCs) - one for the cupolas, another for the casemates and a third for *Bloc V* and *Coupole Sud*. The fort's operational chain of command was based on the deployment of the field army with different units directing the fire of Eben-Emael's guns at targets within their area of responsibility. Following the September 1939 mobilisation Eben-Emael came within the area of operations of *I Corps d'Armée* (I CA), which was responsible for the defence of the southern portion of the Albert Canal Line. Administratively the fort remained under the command of III CA that was tasked with the defence of Liège. In May 1940 target orders for *Coupole 120* were the responsibility of

the I CA; the *7e Division d'Infanterie* (7 DI) directed the fire of *Coupole Nord* and *Coupole Sud*; the *18e Régiment d'Infanterie de Ligne* directed *Maastricht 1* and *Maastricht 1*; the *2e Régiment des Grenadiers* gave fire orders for *Visé 1*; and, the commander of the Secteur Meuse-Aval directed the guns of *Visé 2*. Fixed targets, such as the Albert Canal bridges, were precisely plotted so that gun crews only had to refer to the coordinates. The government's policy of neutrality did not permit any fire to be directed into Dutch territory. Eben-Emael's commander was responsible for destroying the bridges at Kanne and Petit Lanaye and the canal locks at Lanaye. The headquarters at Lanaeken was responsible for the demolition of the Vroenhoven and Veltwezelt bridges.

Eben-Emael was more powerful than any single *gros ouvrage* (big fort) on the Maginot Line. Many lessons of World War One were incorporated in its design such as the dispersal of the fighting emplacements, better protection for the ammunition magazines, arrangements to seal off any position that was captured and an elaborate air filtration system to protect against gas attack.

Nevertheless, in comparison with the French forts some economies were apparent including the decision not to provide railways or lifts to move personnel within Eben-Emael despite its great size. The fort was well protected from external attack but when it was designed in 1932 little thought was given to the possibility of an enemy landing on top of the fort; there was little barbed wire to impede movement inside the fort and no trenches for

Left: *Canal Nord*, a machine gun bunker on the east bank of the Albert Canal. Note the armoured observation cupola. *(FE-E)*

internal defence. Air defences were weak because the designers believed that the small emplacements, skilfully blended into the terrain, would be difficult to hit from the air and that no bomb could penetrate their massive armour.

During the 1914-18 the garrisons of Belgian forts included infantry units that provided close defence. However, in the interwar period this doctrine was changed so that the close defence of forts became the responsibility of the field army. Eben-Emael's garrison was drawn entirely from the *Régiment de Forteresse de Liège* (RFL), a fortress artillery unit formed in 1930 whose soldiers received no training in infantry tactics. By May 1940 the RFL consisted of a regimental headquarters at Liège and five groups, each of which was organised into two to five fortress batteries. The *1er Groupe*, consisting of two batteries, was assigned to Eben-Emael under the command of Major Jean Fritz Lucien Jottrand. At full strength the garrison should have numbered 1,322 personnel including about 300 headquarters and support staff. As it was unhealthy and detrimental to morale to spend long periods underground the garrison was divided into two shifts of about 500 each that would man the gun emplacements for one-week rotations. The shift not on duty was billeted in the village of Wonck

and with no allocated transport it usually took 6km (3.73 miles) to march from Wonck to the fort. The headquarters and support staff was either billeted in two wooden barrack blocks outside the fort's entrance or in the nearby village of Eben-Emael. On 10 May 1940 the garrison was reduced by a combination of undermanning, sickness and leave to a total strength of only 883 men.

For the officers there was little prestige in serving with a fortress artillery unit. After the September 1939 mobilisation the fort's under-strength peacetime garrison was reinforced by reservists from the 1929, 1931 and 1935 intakes who had no previous experience with the 75mm Model 1934 guns or the 60mm Model 1936 anti-tank guns. Conscripts from the '1940 class' were posted to the RFL upon completion of their initial training without passing through the *Dépot de renfort et d'instruction* (Reinforcement and training depot) and had spent only three months in uniform. The RFL included personnel who were not considered fit for field service because of minor medical problems while soldiers who were the fathers of large families were posted to the fort to be near their homes. Undermanning, inadequate training, poor cohesion and a growing ennui as the Phoney War dragged on undermined the morale of the Eben-Emael garrison.

Above: **Bloc-01** **located above the Albert Canal on the southern end of the fort.** *(FE-E)*

Right: **The position as it was in 1940, photographed from the site of Lanaye locks.** *(JSS)*

Above: **A view along the anti-tank ditch towards *Bloc V*. (JSS)**

Left: **The main tunnel under the fort from the entrance at *Bloc I*. (F-E-E)**

ARMAMENT OF FORT EBEN-EMAEL 10 MAY 1940

[designation assigned by German intelligence]

1er Batterie

Coupole 120   [Werk 24]
Two 120mm guns (360⁰ arc)
One SNCO, three JNCOs and 24 privates

Coupole Nord   [Werk 31]
Two 75mm guns (360⁰ arc)
One SNCO, two JNCOs and 22 privates

Coupole Sud   [Werk 23]
Two 75mm guns (360⁰ arc)
One light machine gun (infantry exit)
One SNCO, two JNCOs and 22 privates

Casemate Maastricht 1 (Ma1)   [Werk 12]
Three 75mm guns (arcs to the north)
One SNCO, four JNCOs and 28 privates

Casemate Maastricht 2 (Ma2)   [Werk 18]
Three 75mm guns (arcs to the north)
One SNCO, four JNCOs and 28 privates

Casemate Visé 1 (Vi1)   [Werk 26]
Three 75mm guns (arcs to the south)
One SNCO, four JNCOs and 28 privates

Casemate Visé 2 (Vi2)   [Werk 9]
Three 75mm guns (arcs to the south)
One SNCO, four JNCOs and 28 privates

2e Batterie

Bloc 1   [Werk 3]
Two 60mm guns (arcs to the west and north)
Three machine guns (arcs to the west, north and south)
One light machine gun (inside entrance)
Two searchlights
One observation cupola
One SNCO, four JNCOs and 23 privates

Right: **The man-made Caster Cut through which the Albert Canal passed. At the end of the cut are Lanaye Locks where the canal joins with the Maas (Meuse) river.** *(FE-E)*

Bloc II   *[Werk 4]*
Two 60mm guns (arcs to the north and south)
Two machine guns (arcs to the north and south)
One light machine gun (infantry exit)
Two searchlights
One observation cupola
Two SNCO, 2 JNCOs and 22 privates

Bloc IV   *[Werk 30]*
Two 60mm guns (arcs to the west and east)
Two machine guns (arcs to the west and east)
Two searchlights
One observation cupola
Two SNCO, 2 JNCOs and 22 privates

Bloc V   *[Werk 23]*
One 60mm gun (arc to the west)
Two machine guns (arcs to the west)
One searchlights
One observation cupola
One SNCO, 2 JNCOs and 14 privates

Bloc VI   *[Werk 6]*
Two 60mm guns (arcs to the west and north)
One machine guns (arcs to the west and north)
One searchlights
One observation cupola
Two SNCO, 1 JNCOs and 17 privates

Canal Nord   *[Werk 17]*
One 60mm gun (arc to the north)
Three machine guns (1 with arc to the north and 2 south)
Two searchlights
One observation cupola with light machine gun
One SNCO, 2 JNCOs and 17 privates

Canal Sud   *[Werk 35]*
One 60mm gun (arc to the south)
Three machine guns (2 with arcs to the north and 1 south)
Two searchlights
One observation cupola with light machine gun
One SNCO, 2 JNCOs and 17 privates

Right: **A 7.65mm Maxim machine gun mounting. This weapon was used in all emplacements except *Visé I* and *II*, *Maastricht MAI* and *MA2* and *Coupole 120*.** *(TG)*

Below: **Details of the mountings for the 75mm FRC Model 1934 as used in *Maastricht* or *Visé* bunkers.** *(TG)*

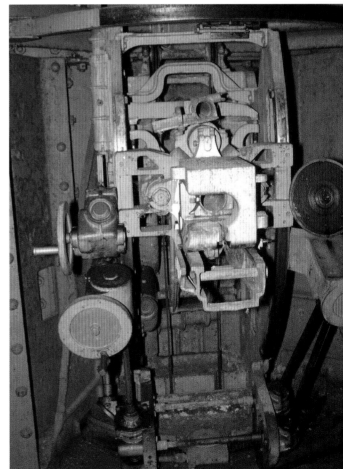

Left: Lanaye locks at the junction of the Maas (Meuse) river and the Albert Canal. At left is the Caster cutting through St. Peter's Mount which was excavated for the route of the canal. *(FE-E)*

Left: The weir for overflow water from the anti-tank ditch. The ditch was filled with water by-passed from the Geer river. Fort Eben-Emael is on the left. *(FE-E)*

Bloc 01   [*Werk 32*]
One 60mm gun (arc to the east)
Three machine guns (one with arcs to the
   north, one north/east and one south)
Two searchlights
One observation cupola
One SNCO, Three JNCOs and 18 privates

Mitrailleuses Nord (MiN)   [*Werk 19*]
Three machine guns (one with arc to the
   north, one east and one south)
Three searchlights
Three JNCOs and 18 privates

Mitrailleuses Sud (MiS)   [*Werk 13*]
Three machine guns (one with arc to the
   north and two south)
Two searchlights
One light machine gun (infantry exit)
Three JNCOs and 18 privates

Mitrailleuses contre avion (MICA) [*Werk 29*]
Four machine guns
One officer, One SNCO, four JNCOs
   and 13 privates

BELGIUM IN ARMS

After the mobilisation of September 1939 Belgium had about 900,000 men under arms. The army was organised into seven *corps d'armée* and a *corps de cavalerie*. The major manoeuvre units comprised 18 infantry divisions, two cavalry divisions and two divisions for the defence of the Ardennes region. In May 1940 five corps with 12 divisions were deployed along the Albert Canal; one corps of two divisions was protecting Liège; another corps of two divisions was protecting the Meuse River from Liège to the French frontier; while a cavalry division and an Ardennais division were deployed in the Ardennes. In accordance with the defensive posture dictated by the government the army had less than 270 light tanks, T-13s armed with a 47mm gun and the 13.2mm T-15 machine gun. These were dispersed in small groups with a typical infantry division assigned 12 T-13s. The Belgian air force was organised into a reconnaissance regiment with about 60 aircraft, a fighter regiment with about 80 aircraft and a bomber regiment with 40 aircraft. Almost 100 of these aircraft were obsolete British-designed Fairey Fox biplane fighters.

2e RÉGIMENT DE GRENADIERS

During the September 1939 mobilisation the Belgian Army reformed the *2e Régiment de Grenadiers* (2nd Grenadier Regiment) from reservists of the classes of 1932, 1933, 1934 and 1935 that had completed their conscript service with *1er Régiment de Grenadiers*. About 80% of the regiment's officers were also reservists.

On April 26 1940 the *2e Grenadiers*, one of the three infantry regiments of the *7e Division d'Infanterie*, received orders to leave the area of Halle - Ninove and take up a new position in the area of Fort Eben-Emael. The 2e Grenadiers were deployed on a 9km front along the Albert Canal with the 2nd Battalion on the left occupying positions from OP Kanne to the village of Eben-Emael and the 3rd Battalion on the right from Loen to Lixhe. The 1st Battalion was positioned in depth in the region Fall – Meer – Wonck. A battery of 105mm self-propelled guns of the *20e Régiment d' Artilleries Motorisé* (20th Motorised Artillery Regiment) was in direct support. Although the *2e Grenadiers* had an establishment of 3,400 personnel its effective strength on 10 May was about 2,600.

7e DIVISION D'INFANTERIE/7TH INFANTRY DIVISION (GENERAL MICHIELS)

2e Régiment de Grenadiers
2e Régiment de Carabiniers
18e Line Regiment
*20e Artillery Regiment**
7e Engineer Battalion

*Attached from the 2nd Chasseurs Ardennes Division in exchange for the 12th Artillery Regiment.

The Regiment General Göring was transferred into the Luftwaffe on 1 October 1935. From volunteers of the regiment, a Parachute Soldiers Battalion was established as a cadre for future Parachute Troops.

3

FALLSCHIRMJÄGER

During a business trip to Germany in 1922 Eddie Rickenbacker, America's 'Ace of Aces' during World War One, was entertained by four former German fighter pilots including Hermann Göring. Rickenbacker later described this meeting in his book *Seven Came Through*:

'Göring said something I still remember. He said: "Our whole future is in the air. And it is by air power that we are going to recapture the German empire. To accomplish this we will do three things. First, we will teach gliding as a sport to all our young men. Then we will build up commercial aviation. Finally we will create the skeleton of a military air force. When the time comes, we will put all three together – and the German empire will be reborn".'

In an effort to cripple Germany's military capability the 1919 Treaty of Versailles stipulated that the German Army could number no more than 100,000 men with no tanks, heavy artillery or general staff; restricted the navy to 15,000 men with 24 capital ships and no submarines; and prohibited Germany from having an air force. The Allied Control Commission saw nothing sinister in the many

Left: **Under training before a 'live' jump. The** *Fallschirmjäger,* **at left, is in full harness and suspended from a static line ready to land on the padded matting.** *(JSS)*

Right:
Fallschirmjäger in training, learning how to collapse the parachute canopy after landing. The training base was set up at Stendal to the west of Berlin. *(JSS)*

gliding clubs that sprang up across Germany throughout the 1920s. To encourage an economic revival the commission relaxed provisions in 1923 to allow German industry to develop aircraft for the civilian market. General Hans von Seeckt, the commander of the *Reichswehr* from 1920 until 1926, welcomed these developments. From his appointment Seeckt worked to circumvent the Versailles Treaty and lay the foundations for the resurgence of German military power. In 1921 he negotiated a secret agreement with the Soviet government to allow Germany to covertly train troops and develop weapons in the Soviet Union.

A Soviet military development that aroused the interest of German observers was the formation of parachute forces. A parachute platoon participated in a Soviet exercise for the first time in 1930 and with the support of Marshal Mikhail Tukhachevski, the visionary commander of the Red Army, this force was rapidly expanded to a brigade that staged demonstration drops during the Moscow Air Days in 1933 and 1934. The following year the Soviet government released newsreel film of an

Right: An instructor watches from the rear-gunner's position as a *Fallschirmjäger* makes a training jump. Note the parachute extraction static line from the parachute pack to the aircraft. *(JSS)*

exercise in which a parachute drop by 1,000 men was followed by transport aircraft landing a further 2,500 paratroopers in the drop zone.

In early 1935, two years after the Nazi Party came to power in Germany, *ReichsKanzler* Adolf Hitler announced that Germany was no longer bound by the 1919 Versailles Treaty. He appointed one of his closest political allies, Hermann Göring, to be the commander of the new air force. Western governments were shocked to learn that the *Luftwaffe* numbered about 20,000 men with more than 1,800 German-built aircraft on the day of its formation. Paramilitary police units were incorporated into the new army; one such unit, the *Landespolizeigruppe* [Land Police Group] *General Göring*, was designated the *Regiment General Göring* on 1 April 1935.

Feldmarschall Göring had been one of the German observers at the 1935 Russian exercise and on 23 September 1935 he signed an order stating: 'The *Regiment General Göring* will be transferred into the *Luftwaffe* on 1 October 1935. From volunteers of the regiment, a *Fallschirmschützen Bataillon* [Parachute Soldiers Battalion] is to be established as a cadre for the future German *Fallschirmtruppen* [Parachute Troops].' More than 600 men volunteered for parachute training and Germany's first parachute battalion, designated the *IV Fallschirmschützen-Bataillon, Regiment General Göring*, was formed under the command of Major Bruno Bräuer.

The *Luftwaffe* opened a parachute school at Stendal, 96km (60miles) west of Berlin, early in 1936 and a platoon from the new parachute battalion participated in its first field exercise that October. Early the next year the *Regiment General Göring* formed a *Luftlande-Bataillon* (air landing battalion) that could be carried to battle by the Ju52/3m transport aircraft. The service was also examining using gliders as a third method of delivering assault troops by air. In March 1937 an experimental glider section was established at Darmstadt under the command of *Leutnant* Walter Kiess to conduct operational trials of the new DFS230 glider.

Aware of the potential of parachute forces, and not wanting to be outshone by the *Luftwaffe*, the *Oberkommando des Heeres* (OKH, Army High Command) asked for volunteers in mid-1936 to form a *Schwere-Fallschirm-Infanterie-Kompanie* (Heavy Parachute Infantry Company). As the army had no parachute school of its own the company underwent parachute training at Stendal.

Above: The Germans, like the British and US, used a static line for parachute extraction. This allowed a 'stick' to be dropped in quick time avoiding the problem of troops being spread over a wide area of the landing zone. *(JSS)*

Above: **A Ju52 towing a DFS 230 glider on an experimental short bracket, which was never used. The glider is the same production model as used in the attack on Eben-Emael.** *(JSS)*

Both the *Luftwaffe* battalion and the army parachute company participated in manoeuvres at Mecklenburg in 1937 when their progress was watched with interest by Hitler. The OKH soon authorised the expansion of the army company to a full battalion.

As the formation of Germany's airborne forces gained momentum so too did Hitler's drive to achieve a 'Greater Germany'. As a plan, designated *Fall Grün* (Plan Green), was developed to annex Czechoslovakia it was decided that the fledgling *Fallschirmtruppen* offered a means to vault the country's border defences. Colonel Kurt Student, then serving as *Inspekteur der Fliegerschulen* (Inspector for Flying Training Schools), was promoted to *Generalmajor* and ordered to group the disparate airborne units into a new force to be combat ready by 15 September. From 1 July 1938 the new formation was designated *7. Flieger-Division*. As the hard-working Student set about organising the new force he also considered a doctrinal split between the army and the air force about how airborne forces should be employed. The *Luftwaffe* believe that the *Fallschirmtruppen* should be used as saboteurs in small units to attack key targets and seize airfields while the army

believed the paratroopers should be used in strength. It was to Student's credit that he developed a force that could be employed successfully in both roles during the 1940 campaign.

To bolster the division's numbers a regiment of the army's *22. Infanterie-Division* and a Nazi Party *Sturmabteilung* (Storm Troopers) regiment were allocated for the forthcoming operation. The *7. Flieger-Division* was declared combat ready on 1 September but the Munich Agreement of that month allowed Hitler to occupy the Sudetenland area of Czechoslovakia without invasion. Nevertheless *Feldmarschall* Göring had the opportunity to demonstrate his new force by using 242 Ju52s to fly troops into the Frudenthal area, the division's *Fall Grün*. For security reasons Student forbade a parachute drop and a glider landing by the few DFS230 then available.

Göring's prestige was high with Hitler and he succeeded in having the army's parachute battalion transferred to the *Luftwaffe* on 1 January 1939. The previous year the *General Göring* battalion had been redesignated as the *1. Bataillon, Fallschirmjäger-Regiment* (1st Battalion, 1st Parachute Regiment). The army unit became the regiment's second battalion,

the *Luftwaffe's Luftlande-Bataillon* became the third battalion and newly promoted *Oberst* Bräuer was given command of the complete *Fallschirmjäger Regiment 1* (FJR/1). The formation of a second regiment was also authorised. The OKH agreed to commit the *22. Infanterie-Division* to the air-landing role for future operations commanded by Student who was appointed *Inspekteur der Fallschirm-und-Luftlandetruppe.*

Generalmajor Student worked energetically to prepare his force for war. Student believed his force was an important element of Germany's *Bewegungskrieg* (manoeuvre warfare) doctrine that employed fast moving combined arms battle groups supported by air power to destroy a slower moving enemy's will to fight without having to engage in the costly attritional battles that characterised World War One.

Although this concept is more popularly described as *Blitzkrieg* (lightning war) the term *Blitzkrieg* was first used by a *Time* magazine journalist during the Polish campaign and

was not officially used by any branch of the *Wehrmacht*. Hitler dismissed the term *Blitzkrieg* as 'a totally nonsensical word'. Plans to employ the *7. Flieger-Division* in the parachute assault role during the annexation of Czechoslovakia in March 1939 were overtaken by a combination of bad weather and rapidly advancing ground forces. When Germany invaded Poland on 1 September 1939 the division was not included in the initial assault wave and a number of airborne operations planned subsequently were aborted when fast-moving armoured units supported by Ju87 Stuka dive bombers captured the objectives. Elements of both *Fallschirmjäger 1* and *2* (FJR/1 and 2) saw combat in Poland employed as motorised infantry. After the fighting ceased on 6 October the *Fallschirmjäger* returned to their barracks in Germany.

On 27 October Student piloted a Fieseler *Storch* (Stork) light aircraft to Berlin's Tempelhof airfield following a summons to report to Hitler at the Reichs Chancellery. Student wrote

Above:
Fallschirmjäger
in action. Note the
cut down helmet
and plain smock. In
the background
are an MG34 crew.
This gun was the
standard heavy
machine gun in
use in the German
army in 1940. *(JSS)*

of the meeting: 'During the discussion which took place Hitler gave his views on how airborne troops should be used. His opinions were explained with clear-sighted lucidity and with his own inimitable persuasiveness. I was astonished at his knowledge of what was virtually a new field – of the potential of gliders in particular. To begin with the *Führer* himself stressed that one had to realise that paratroops and the airborne arm was a completely new, untried and – so far as Germany was concerned – still secret weapon. The first airborne operation had to employ every resource available, and be delivered boldly at decisive time and place. It was for this reason, Hitler said, he had refrained from using airborne troops until there were appropriate objectives. I told him of the paratroops disappointment and frustration during the campaign in Poland, and of the effect on their morale. Hitler listened attentively and responded by saying "They will certainly see some action in the West!" Smiling, he added, "And it will be a big show!"'

Hitler showed the general a map covering the Maastricht Appendix, a finger-like projection of territory that points south from the Netherlands to separate Belgium from Germany. The strip is only 24km (14.9 miles) across at its widest point through the city of Maastricht. Running along the west of the Appendix inside the Belgian border was one of the newest features on the map - the 130km (81.78miles) long Albert Canal that had been completed that year. Ostensibly built to provide a Belgian route to link Liège with Antwerp it also provided a formidable obstacle blocking a German invasion through Belgium into France. The major routes from Maastricht into Belgium crossed the canal over new bridges at Veldwezelt, Vroenhoven and Kanne. The other significant new feature was Fort Eben-Emael built by the Belgians to protect the bridges over the Albert Canal to the north and the Meuse River to the south.

Hitler showed Student air photographs of the fort and explained: 'The top is like a large grassy field. It has some surface fortifications – I have reports there are heavy artillery gun cupolas and casemates – some machine guns.'

After remarking on Student's long experience with gliders and his personal interest in

the development of the DFS230, Hitler stated: 'I have an idea. I think some of your attack gliders could land on top of Fort Eben-Emael and your men could storm these works. Is that possible?' Student asked time to consider the proposal.

Student understood that surprise and speed were essential if the scheme was to have any chance of success. The noise and slow speed of the Ju52 would make a stealthy approach impossible. It was difficult to drop paratroopers on a precise point and even in ideal conditions a stick of 12 *Fallschirmjäger* jumping from the minimum height of 90m (295ft) would be spread over more than 250m (820ft). They would then have to reach their weapon and equipment canisters before they could begin their mission. In contrast, the DFS230 could deliver 10 men and their equipment silently over a distance of 20km and a good pilot could easily land well within 50m (164ft) of an objective.

The following day Student told Hitler that he believed that up to 12 gliders could be landed successfully on Eben-Emael with the provision that the attack be made in daylight or morning twilight. At this second meeting Hitler revealed that German scientists had secretly developed a new weapon that could be used to duplicate the explosive force of the 420mm shells that smashed the Liège forts in 1914. He explained that the *Hohlladungwaffe* (hollow-charge explosive) could blow a hole through any known fortifications but that the demolition charge needed to be placed by hand. Hitler directed Student to immediately begin planning for a glider assault to capture Eben-Emael and stressed that all aspects of planning and preparation be conducted in the strictest secrecy. On 29 October Student received written orders to begin detailing planning for a glider assault to seize the fort and the three Albert Canal bridges thus securing a route for German ground forces. Hitler intended to launch a Western offensive before the end of 1939.

Left: **A** *Luftwaffe* **junior officer wearing the standard issue** *Fliegerbluse* **(flying blouse) that was adopted by the** *Fallschirmjäger.* *(JSS)*

PARACHUTE TRAINING

Fallschirmjäger volunteers received eight weeks of training. The first four weeks was an intensive basic training package modelled on the infantry training syllabus with an additional emphasis on physical toughening. Those who passed the first phase proceeded to four weeks of parachute training that culminated in the award of 'wings' after the successful completion of six parachute jumps. Although the first jump was usually from an altitude of 250m (820ft) most training jumps were from the operational altitude of 120m (400ft). To achieve as tight a concentration on the ground as possible a stick of 12 paratroopers had to exit a Ju-52 in just 30 seconds.

CLOTHING AND EQUIPMENT

The men of *Sturmabteilung Koch* were equipped essentially the same as their comrades in *7. Flieger-Division* who parachuted into Holland on the same day. *Fallschirmjäger* wore a blue short waisted, open necked *Luftwaffe* flying blouse with buttons hidden under a fly front. The officers' *Fliegerbluse* was worn with shirt and tie. The *Fallschirmjäger* trousers had two side pockets, two hip pockets and a small 'fob' pocket on the front of the right hip. There were slits, closed by press fasteners, on the side seams outside of the knee to allow kapok-filled canvas kneepads to be inserted to provide protection during parachute jumps. Behind the slit on the right leg was a pocket, closed by three fasteners, for a single-bladed gravity knife that could be used to cut away parachute rigging in an emergency. The knife was held pointing downward and a push button released the blade; when the button was released the blade was locked. The trousers were gathered at the ankle by tapes and buttons. *Fallschirmjäger* were issued with black ankle-length jump boots (*Fallschirmschnürschuhe*) that laced on the outside of the instep. These had thick rubber soles and were not fitted with the hobnails as standard on *Wehrmacht* boots.

Members of *Sturmabteilung* Koch wore the 'first pattern' *Luftwaffe* smock made of a windproof grey/green gabardine cotton drill material. This had two tailored legs that extended to a point midway between the hip and the knee and a zipper that reached from the crotch to the throat. Photographs of the officers show variations in the pocket arrangements: *Hauptmann* Koch had a zippered cargo pocket on each thigh while *Oberleutnant* Witzig

Right: The same officer, this time in flying kit for glider pilots and at far left in dress cap and tunic. The insignia for glider pilots is the same stylised seagull but on a yellow patch instead of red. *(JSS)*

did not. For parachute operations the wearer stepped into the smock and pulled it on over his equipment so that there was no risk of snagged equipment preventing the parachute from deploying properly. After landing a *Fallschirmjäger* removed his smock and equipment and then buckled the equipment over the smock. This cumbersome procedure was not necessary for gliderborne operations as troops were dressed ready for immediate action.

Rank patches, similar to those worn by *Luftwaffe* aircrew on their flying suits, were beginning to be worn on the sleeves of the smock in May 1940 however none of the officers photographed with Hitler is wearing these patches. In such a small, well-trained group these rank distinctions would not have been necessary.

An item of clothing unique to the *Fallschirmjäger* was the soft, black leather *Handschuhe* (gauntlets) that were elasticated at wrist and cuff. Designed to keep the hands warm inside the unheated Ju52 cabin and during the parachute drop, these provided useful protection at Eben-Emael.

The grey *Fallschirmjäger* helmet was originally made by cutting the brim from

a standard German helmet and helmets were later produced in this pattern. The *Fallschirmjäger* helmet had a more extensive harness and the interior was padded. The national black-white-red shield was painted on the right side of the helmet and a *Luftwaffe* eagle on the left. Camouflage helmet covers were not worn at this stage of the war and the members of *Koch* heavily smeared their helmets with mud before the operation so that these insignia are not apparent in photographs.

In photographs the men of *Sturmgruppe Granit* are wearing a stripped down version of the basic load carrying equipment: a leather belt, Y-straps, automatic pistol holster on the left hip, gasmask bag, 'breadbag' and canteen behind the right hip. *Fallschirmjäger* armed with the MP38/40 submachine gun carried a set of triple magazine pouches on the belt. Those armed with the *Karabinier* (Kar) 98K carbine carried a cloth bandolier around the neck which hung down both sides of the chest and had loops to anchor it to the waist belt on either side of the buckle. The bandolier's twelve press-fastened compartments held 120 rounds. The sappers of *Granit* carried 74 torches and in later accounts mentioned how useful these were in the smoke filled interiors of

Fallschirmjäger on exercise. The troops are wearing the standard helmet and jumpsuit, also the black ankle-length jump boots (*Fallshirmschnür-schühe*) and the soft leather gauntlets (*Hand-shühe*). The officer leading would be armed with a *Machinen pistole* (MP 38/40). The troops are carrying Mauser Kar98 carbines and are followed by an MG34 machine gun crew. *(JSS)*

Left: Hitler with the surviving *Trupp* leaders from *Sturmabteilung Koch. Major* (newly promoted from *Hauptmann*) Koch is to the right of Hitler. *Oberleutnant* Rudolf Witzig, commander of the *Pionierzug* (pioneer [sapper]) platoon. *(BA)*

Below: The beginnings of *Fallschirmjäger*, on parade in Berlin, are members of *7 Flieger-Division* which was declared operational on 1 September 1939. The soldier nearest the camera wears parachutist wings. *(AN)*

GERMAN RANKS AND BRITISH EQUIVALENTS

Generalfeldmarschall	Field Marshal
Generaloberst	General
General der Fallschirmtruppe	General
Generalleutnant	Lieutenant General
Generalmajor	Major General
Oberst	Colonel
Oberstleutnant	Lieutenant Colonel
Major	Major
Hauptmann	Captain
Oberleutnant	Lieutenant
Leutnant	2nd Lieutenant
Stabsfeldwebel	Warrant Officer
Oberfeldwebel	Colour Sergeant
Feldwebel	Sergeant
Unterfeldwebel	Lance Sergeant
Oberjäger	Corporal
Hauptgefreiter	Lance Corporal (six years' service)
Obergefreiter	Lance Corporal (two years' service)
Gefreiter	Lance Corporal (six months' service)
Jäger	Private

Eben-Emael's emplacements. These were usually worn clipped to a front webbing strap.

In their accounts of the operation most members of *Granit* recalled that thirst was a problem. *Trupp 3* leader *Oberjäger* Peter Arent, noted in his after action report that his troop had nothing to eat during the action at Eben-Emael and only one water bottle to drink. *Feldwebel* Nidermeier, who led *Trupp 1*, noted in his report that it was impractical to carry two waterbottles. In the heavily loaded gliders weight was at a premium and rations were not thought necessary as the plan called for the force to be relieved within six hours. Some of the sappers carried chocolate bars and cigarettes.

WEAPONS

In 1940 the *Fallschirmjäger* used standard issue *Wehrmacht* small arms and support weapons; compact weapon variants and weapons developed for use by airborne troops appeared later in the war. The majority of *Granit's* junior ranks carried the Kar 98k carbine while *Trupp* leaders and other NCOs carried the MP40 sub-machine gun. Its compact size and high rate of fire made the MP40 an ideal weapon when the *Fallschirmjäger* entered Eben-Emael's emplacements but also for driving off the half-hearted Belgian counterattacks. The group's most effective weapons were six MG34s. The MG34 was one of the most successful machine gun designs of the 20th century that could be used in the light machine gun role or mounted on a tripod to provide sustained fire. Fed from 50-round belts it had a rate of fire of 1,550 rounds per minute and a muzzle velocity of 755m (2,475ft) per second.

Sturmgruppe Granit was equipped with five *Flammenwerfer* (flamethrowers) but there is disagreement among sources as to whether these were the *Flammenwerfer 35*, the standard model at the start of war, or prototypes of the lighter *Flammenwerfer 40*. *Oberfeldwebel* Portsteffen's platoon from *Pionierbataillon 51*, the first elements of the relief force to reach Eben-Emael on 11 May, used the *Modell 35* to attack *Bloc II* overlooking the wet moat. This weighed 35.8kg (78.9lb) when it was loaded with 11.8 litres of oil (2.6gal). It could fire a single jet of flame up to 30m (98ft) long for a maximum of 10 seconds although depending upon the target, shorter bursts of

one of two seconds were usually used. The *Modell 40* weighed 21.8kg (48.1lb) with a 7.5-litre (1.6gal) oil tank. After some modifications this went into production as the *Flammenwerfer 41*.

To knock out Eben-Emael's fortifications *Sturmgruppe Granit* carried more than 2,408kg (5,308lb) of explosives distributed in its 11 gliders. The 50kg and 12.5kg *Hohlladungwaffen* represented 1,750kg (3,858lb) of this total. The force also carried conventional 3kg (6.6lb) and 1kg (2.2lb) demolition charges, *Stielhandgranate 24* 'stick' grenades and lighter *Eihandgranate 39* 'egg' hand grenades. These were stuffed through the periscopes and embrasures and dropped down stairwells once the emplacements had been breached. Witzig's sappers also built one 6m (19.7ft) and three 4m (13.1ft) ladders to scale the walls of the fort's anti-tank ditch.

HOHLLADUNGWAFFE

The secret weapon that Hitler believed would allow a glider-borne assault force to neutralise Fort Eben-Emael was the *Hohlladungwaffe* (hollow-charge weapon).

American chemist Charles Munroe first described the principle of the hollow charge while working at the US Naval Torpedo Station, Newport, Rhode Island in the 1880s. When Munroe detonated blocks of explosives against steel plates representing the armour of warships he noticed that the initials 'USN' inscribed on the blocks were reproduced on the plates. The high pressures of the explosion were directed towards the cavity to produce a very high overpressure against the target. Munroe found that by deepening the cavity on the

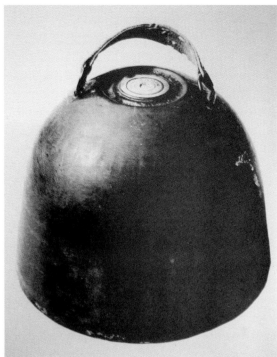

Left: **The 12.5kg** *Hohlladungwaffe* **(hollow-charge weapon) used to great effect at Eben-Emael. A** *Sprengskapsel Nr. 8* **igniter was fitted in the cap. The weapon was carried by the webbing handle at the top.** *(TG)*

Far Left: **A 3kg demolition charge with ZZ.35 igniters in position.** *(TG)*

explosive charge he could increase the penetration of the target. This became known as the 'Munroe Effect' in Britain and the USA. In Germany the principle was called the 'Neumann Effect' after an engineer who demonstrated on the eve of World War One that a cylinder of explosives with a hollow conical cavity could achieve better penetration of steel plate than a solid cylinder of explosives.

Throughout the 1920s and 1930s the German Army's *Waffenamt Prufwesen* (Offices of Weapons Proof and Development) conducted research on military applications of the 'Neumann Effect' and by 1939 the department had developed a 12.5kg (27.6lb) and a 50kg (110.2lb) *Hohlladungwaffe*. This was a simple beehive-shaped block of explosive with a hemispherical cavity in the base. They were encased in a sheet iron container. The smaller charge came in one piece while the 50kg charge was produced in two sections that were screwed together. Each charge or section was fitted with a web carrying handle. The *Hohlladungwaffe* was detonated using a 10-second delay *Sprengskapsel Nr.8* igniter inserted in the top of the charge. *Sturmgruppe Granit* was equipped with 26 of the 12.5kg and 28 of the 50kg *Hohlladungwaffen*.

The *Hohlladungwaffe* lacked two refinements necessary to maximise the effectiveness of the 'Munroe Effect'. A 'modern' shaped charge employs a 'stand off' method to detonate the charge at the correct distance from the target to maximise the armour-piercing effect. The charge also has a cone-shaped cavity that is lined with a thin sheet of metal such as copper, zinc or steel. When the charge or warhead is detonated the pressure waves converge to produce a thin column of intense flame that burns a small hole through steel, concrete or other materials. The liner melts to form a slug of molten metal that converges on the axis of the explosion to follow the flame jet to increase the destructive effect. If the diameter of the warhead, angle of the cone liner and the standoff distance are correct the resulting slug can travel at velocities of 10,000m/sec (32,808ft/sec) enabling it to penetrate solid steel armour equal to 150-250% of the warhead diameter.

EXPLOSIVES CARRIED BY STURMGRUPPE GRANIT

Explosive	Total weight
28 50kg *Hohlladungwaffe*	1,400kg (3,086.4lb)
28 12.5kg *Hohlladungwaffe*	350kg (771.6lb)
83 3kg charges	249kg (549lb)
106 1kg charges	106kg (234lb)
nine 6kg pole charges	54kg (119lb)
eight boxes containing 25kg of explosives	200kg (440lb)
33 1.5kg 'tube explosive' charges	50kg (110lb)

Right: **The 50kg *Hohlladungwaffe* with the igniter in position. It was carried by two webbing handles. At the base is the hole (plugged) for filling with the explosive.** *(TG)*

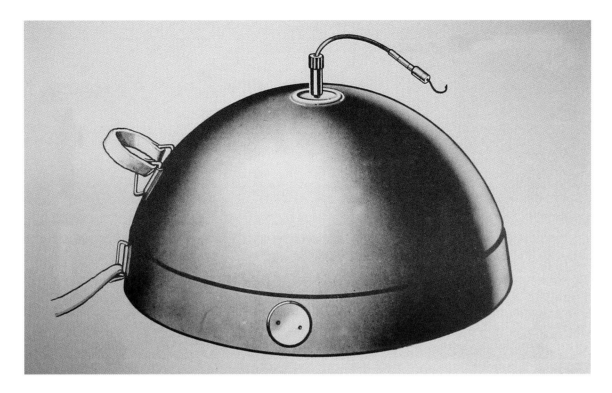

Below: **Damage caused by a single *Hohlladungwaffe* on the false cupola at the north corner of Fort Eben-Emael.** *(FE-E))*

The *Hohlladungwaffe* had no lining and was placed directly on the target. The 12.5kg charge could penetrate up to 120mm (4.73in) of armour and the 50kg charge up to 254mm (10in) of armour although neither achieved this degree of penetration on Eben-Emael's cupolas because of the high-quality steel used in their construction. The *Hohlladungwaffe* proved more successful against the thinner armour of the observation cupolas than the larger, more heavily armoured gun cupolas. Although no charges fully penetrated the target they nevertheless produced tremendous

shock waves that forced destructive flakes of metal to break off of the internal face of the cupolas and ricochet inside causing considerable damage. This 'spalling' effect is comparable to that produced by modern high-explosive squash-head tank ammunition.

Eben-Emael's fighting casemates and cupolas were neutralised by the combination of multiple *Hohlladungwaffen* being exploded against a single target and the use of conventional demolition charges. *Unteroffizier* Karl-Heinz Lange detonated a 50kg *Hohlladungwaffe* on the dome of *Coupole 120* without impeding its

Left: **The Maschinen-pistole 38/40 (MP38/40) carried by the leaders and senior NCOs in the Fallschirmjäger.** *(TG)*

operation. The cupola was neutralised when *Oberfeldwebel* Helmut Wenzel exploded a 3kg demolition charge in each gun barrel. *Feldwebel* Erwin Haug detonated a 50kg charge on *Coupole Sud* and then moved on to attack other positions. The explosion damaged *Coupole Sud* but nevertheless its two 75mm guns remained in action until Eben-Emael surrendered. Although its design was comparatively inefficient the use of the *Hohlladungwaffe* produced a tremendous psychological impact on the morale of the Belgian defenders.

True shaped-charge warheads were used later in the war by anti-tank weapons such as the German *Panzerfaust*, the British Projector Infantry Anti-Tank (PIAT) and the US Army's 2.36in Bazooka.

Hohlladungwaffe dimensions		
Weight:	12.5kg (26.56lb)	50kg (110.23lb)
Outside diameter:	279mm (11in)	508mm (20in)
Cavity diameter:	135mm (5.42in)	203mm (8in)

Below: **The MG34 was one of the most successful machine gun designs of the war. The weapon was fitted as shown with a bipod mounting but could be mounted on a special tripod (see page 30) for more sustained fire.** *(TG)*

WEAPONS CARRIED BY *STURMGRUPPE GRANIT*

Sauer-Selbstladerpistole Modell 38H (pistol)

Calibre:	7.65mm
Length:	171mm (6.74in)
Barrel length:	83mm (3.27in)
Magazine capacity:	eight rounds
Muzzle velocity:	274m/sec (898.9ft/sec)
Rate of fire:	single-shot

Machinenpistole 38/40 (MP38/40) sub-machine gun

Calibre:	9mm
Length:	833mm (33in) with stock extended 630mm (24.8in) with stock folded
Barrel length:	251mm
Magazine capacity:	32 rounds
Weight with loaded magazine:	4.7kg (10.36lb)
Maximum effective range:	200m (219yd)
Muzzle velocity:	365m/sec (805ft/sec)
Rate of fire:	500rpm

Karabiner 98K (Kar98K carbine)

Calibre:	7.92mm
Length:	1,075mm (42.36in)
Barrel length:	600mm (23.64in)
Magazine capacity:	five rounds
Weight with loaded magazine:	3.9kg (8.6lb)
Maximum effective range:	800m (875yd)
Muzzle velocity:	755m/sec (2,477ft/sec)
Rate of fire:	15rpm single-shot

Maschinengewehr 34 (MG34 machine gun)

Calibre:	7.92mm
Length:	1,219mm (48in)
Barrel length:	627mm (24.7in)
Weight:	10.5kg (23.15lb)
Feeding:	50 or 250 round belts 75 round double drum magazine.
Muzzle velocity:	755m/sec (2,477ft/sec)
Rate of fire:	900rpm

Above: **The standard issue Kar 98K rifle must have been a cumbersome weapon for** *Fallschirmjäger* **when exiting the DFS 230 glider.** *(TG)*

Weapon	Ammunition per weapon	Total Ammunition
six 7.92mm MG34 machine guns	1,550 rounds plus 600 reserve	12,900 rounds
18 9mm MP38/40 sub-machine guns	10 x 32 round magazines	5,760 rounds
58 7.92mm Mauser Kar98K carbines	110 rounds	5,940 rounds
85 7.65mm Sauer Modell 38H pistols	64 rounds	5,440 rounds
five 27mm Walther *Leuchpistole* (flare pistol)	50 white, 50 green and 50 red flares	150 flares
Stielhandgranate 24 grenade	424	
Eihandgranate 39 grenade	106	
smoke grenades	106	
smoke charges	53	

Left: The standard issue pistol to *Fallschirmjäger* was the *Sauer Modell 38,* a compact weapon of 7.65mm calibre. *(TG)*

Below: The *Walther 27mm Leuchpistole* (flare pistol) was used by *Fallschirmjäger* at Eben-Emael for signalling to aircraft. *(TG)*

COMMUNICATIONS

Landing at separate locations, dependent upon close air support and awaiting relief from ground forces advancing more than 25km (15.5 miles) over separate routes, communications would have been an important planning consideration for *Hauptmann* Koch. Yet surprisingly little mention is made of this vital command and control function in either contemporary or secondary accounts of the operation. Each group was equipped with at least one battery operated *Modell b1* radio. With a range of 10km (6.2 miles) in the radio telephone (R/T) mode and 25km (15.5 miles) in the wireless/telegraph

Right: The *Panzerbüsche 38/39* anti-tank fitment to the Kar 98K rifle. The weapon was used to disable two Belgian T-13 light tanks in a counter-attack against Veltwezelt bridge. *(TG)*

Right: The *Stielhandgranate* known to Allied troops as the 'potato masher'. *(TG)*

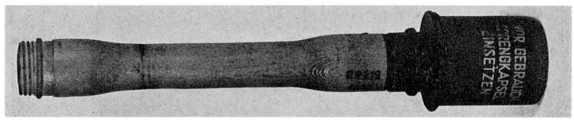

Right: The *Eihandgranate*, egg shaped handgrenade. *(TG)*

(W/T mode) the *Modell b1* was normally used at the battalion and regimental level during conventional operations. The smaller *Modell d2* used at company level had an R/T range of only 4km (2.49 miles) and a W/T range of 15km (9.32 miles). *Oberleutnant* Witzig, *Leutnant* Delica

and *Oberfeldwebel* Wenzel travelled in separate gliders to Eben-Emael to increase the chances of at least one senior commander arriving on the objective. Surprisingly none was accompanied by radios as *Sturmgruppe Granit's* two radio operators both landed in Glider 10. Communications during the operation were comparatively smooth as *Hauptmann* Koch's headquarters, located with *Sturmgruppe Beton* at Vroenhoven bridge, established radio contact with the other assault groups within 30 minutes of landing.

The glider forces were not entirely dependent on radios for communications with the Ju87 pilots as each group carried Nazi flags, air recognition panels and signal pistols. Both at Eben-Emael and at the bridges the *Fallschirmjäger* quickly laid out flags or recognition panels in the shape of a swastika when they captured an emplacement. These panels could also be used to indicate that a squad was fighting on a position, that a position should be bombed and that an ammunition resupply was required. The assault groups were also equipped with the 27mm Walther *Leuchpistole* (flare pistol). Green flares were used to indicate friendly positions, red flares enemy positions and white flares were used to provide illumination at night.

Sturmabteilung Koch was formed and trained in great secrecy using titles such as a trials battalion or airfield construction platoon.

4

PLANNING AND PREPARATION

Generalmajor Student wasted no time following his meeting with Hitler on 28 October. After discussing the proposed operation with *Oberst* Bräuer, commander of FJR 1, Student decided to form a special assault force under the command of *Hauptmann* Walter Koch, a company commander in I/FJR 1 who was noted for determination and thoroughness. The 29-year-old Koch had served in the *Landespolizeigruppe General Göring* and the *General Göring Regiment* before volunteering to become one of Germany's first *Fallschirmjäger*. The core of Koch's force consisted of his own

company and *Oberleutnant* Rudolf Witzig's *Pionierzug* (pioneer platoon) from II/FJR 1.

The 23-year-old Witzig had joined the army in 1935 and served with *Pionierbataillon 16* before being commissioned in 1937. He completed his parachute training in 1938. The experimental glider pilot section commanded by *Leutnant* Kiess, one of the first two *Luftwaffe* pilots trained to fly the DFS 230 glider in 1938, was assigned to the force. When it was fully assembled *Sturmabteilung Koch* (Assault Group Koch) comprised 11 officers and 427 other ranks including 42 glider pilots. It was initially

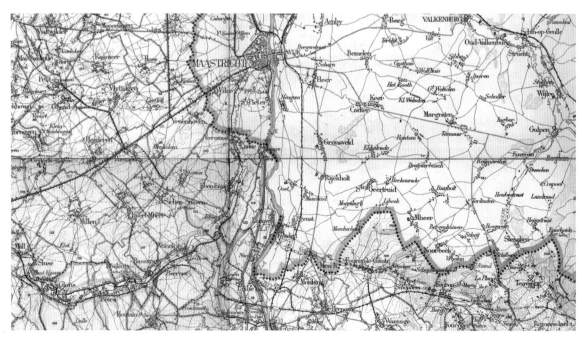

Left: **A Belgian Army map dating from 1925 showing the country's frontier drawn after 1918. The Albert Canal and Fort Eben-Emael are yet to be built** *(JSS)*

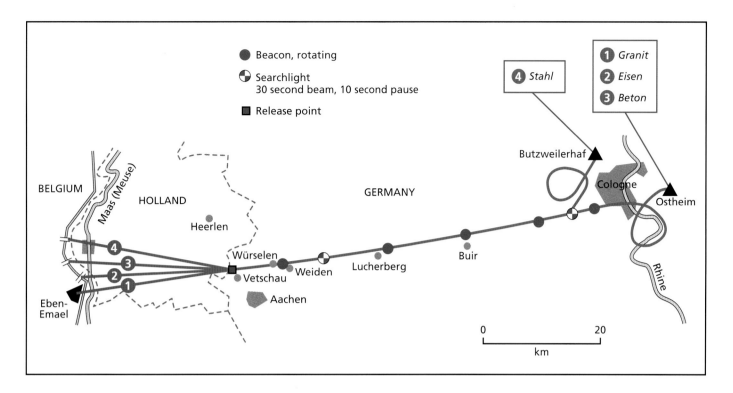

Beacon, rotating

Searchlight
30 second beam, 10 second pause

Release point

1 Granit
2 Eisen
3 Beton

4 Stahl

BELGIUM

Maas (Meuse)

HOLLAND

GERMANY

Heerlen

Butzweilerhaf

Cologne

Ostheim

Würselen

Vetschau

Weiden

Lucherberg

Buir

Rhine

Eben-
Emael

Aachen

0   20

km

Above: **The flight plan for the attack on 10 May 1940.**

Below: **A schematic of the flight plan showing flight time, distance and altitude.**

based at Hildesheim, in the Harz mountains in northern Germany.

Koch was given his detailed orders from Student on 3 November. He formed his unit into four assault groups each with a specific objective:

Sturmgruppe Eisen (Iron), led by *Leutnant* Martin Schaechter, was to capture and hold the Kannes bridge carrying the Maastricht-Liège road. The force comprised 90 men and 10 gliders.

Sturmgruppe Stahl (Steel), under the command of *Oberleutnant Gustav* Altmann, was to seize and hold the Veltwezelt bridge carrying

the Maastricht-Antwerp road. The force comprised 92 men to be carried in 9 gliders.

Sturmgruppe Beton (Concrete), commanded by *Oberleutnant* Gerhard Schacht, was to capture and hold the Vroenhoven bridge carrying the Maastricht-Brussels road. The force numbered 96 men and 10 gliders. Another glider would carry Koch's command team.

Sturmgruppe Granit (Granite), led by Witzig, would seize Eben-Emael, destroy any guns that threatened the bridges and hold its position until relieved by advancing ground forces. The 86-strong force would be carried in 11 gliders.

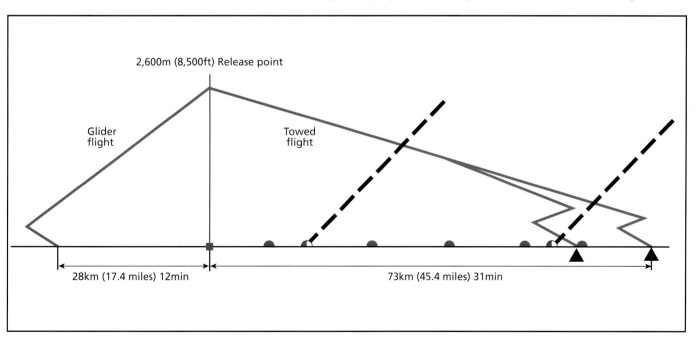

2,600m (8,500ft) Release point

Glider
flight

Towed
flight

28km (17.4 miles) 12min

73km (45.4 miles) 31min

To assist in defending the bridges the three assault groups would each be reinforced by a group of 24 or 25 machine gunners that would drop by parachute about 40 minutes after the glider landings. This would be followed by an ammunition resupply drop. Flights of Ju87s would attack selected targets, such as head-quarters and troop concentrations, and would be available to provide close support of the assault groups. The invasion timetable specified that the four groups would be relieved within six hours.

Surprise was crucial to the success of the operation and strict security was enforced throughout the planning and preparation phase. *Sturmabteilung Koch* was originally given the cover name Friedrichshafen Trials Battalion and Witzig's sub-unit was also given a series of cover names, such as Airfield Construction Platoon, to disguise its true purpose. Rank insignia was removed. Until the eve of the assault only Koch and his platoon commanders knew the names of the objective. The men were not allowed to send mail or make telephone calls. The seriousness of the mission was impressed on the *Fallschirmjäger* when they were ordered to sign a declaration stating: 'I am aware that I shall risk sentence of death should I, by intent or carelessness, make known to another person by spoken word or illustration anything concerning the base at which I am serving.' Two men who committed an indiscretion with some local girls were sentenced to death but were allowed to participate in the operation and were subsequently reprieved.

Intelligence was pieced together from a variety of sources such as air photos taken covertly during Lufthansa flights, picture postcards, information supplied by two German companies that worked as sub-contractors during the construction of Eben-Emael and information gleaned from Belgian deserters. This intelligence was used to build accurate table models of the fort and the target bridges. The fort's emplacements were assigned identifying numbers; for example, *Coupole 120* was designated *Werk 24*.

Witzig's task was the most daunting and it was understood that his small force could not capture the complete fort especially as the Germans believed the garrison to be at full strength. For much of the preparation period *Sturmgruppe Granit* conducted an independent training programme. At the Hildesheim training area

Witzig laid out the dimensions of the undisclosed objective and his force developed the tactics and precise sequence for their assault. To achieve his mission Witzig decided that his force must neutralise the anti-aircraft machine gun battery and other machine gun emplacements that could impede the movement of his sappers, destroy the heavy gun emplacements that threatened the canal bridges and destroy the observation cupolas in order to blind the defenders. Each of the 11 gliders would carry a complete squad; nine squads were given primary and secondary objectives while the remaining two were tasked as reserve elements that could take the place of any squad that failed to reach the objective. The failure of German intelligence to detect the true purpose of the fort's three dummy cupolas meant that the two northern emplacements were included among the group's priority objectives.

Sturmgruppe Granit was instructed on the principles of fortress construction at the army's sapper school at Karlshorst and trained on a section of Czechoslovakia's uncompleted Beneš Line in the Sudetenland. France had assisted with the Beneš Line by allowing Czech engineers to study the Maginot Line and loaning one of the designers of the French defences to assist when construction began in 1936. Although the Czech fortifications differed from Eben-Emael in points of detail they nevertheless provided a close approximation on which the German sappers practised assault and demolition techniques. The platoon later trained in Poland to further develop its procedures using the modern fortifications.

Witzig's men practised extensively with the *Modell 35 Flammenwerfer* (flamethrower) and a variety of demolition charges. It was not until January 1940 that they began training with the *Hohlladungwaffe*. In order to maintain secrecy live charges were only detonated against the ground where the effectiveness of the hollow charge against steel and concrete were not apparent. Only Witzig appreciated that this was the 'secret weapon' expected to render Eben-Emael defenceless. The heavy weight of the charges further reinforced the need for fitness. Witzig later said that the physical training his men underwent 'was very demanding and I tried not to concentrate on soccer and things like that, but on climbing with full gear and running with simulated charges. It was tactically oriented.'

Right: **By 1937 more than 40,000 Germans had trained as glider pilots and many of this number were to become the backbone of the Luftwaffe.** *(PJ)*

Sturmabteilung Koch made repeated training flights with fully loaded gliders both to familiarise the paratroopers with the experience of glider flight and to ensure the pilots fully understood the handling characteristics of the DFS 230. The *Fallschirmjäger* quickly learned the importance of securely lashing their equipment to the glider's steel framework so that it did not shift in flight and damage the aircraft or cause injuries during the inevitable rough landing. This was particularly true for Witzig's platoon which was to carry lots of explosives, heavy flamethrowers and assault ladders for its mission.

An early concern for Koch was the individual skills of the DFS 230 pilots, particularly those assigned to *Granit* who were required to land within metres of their objectives. Used to landing on prepared runways, many of the pilots overshot their objectives when landing on natural terrain. Koch contacted the DFS Institute for assistance and two test pilots were sent to assist with the training programme. It was subsequently decided to 'invite' a number of accomplished sport glider pilots to 'volunteer' to join the Luftwaffe and most of these pilots were assigned to *Sturmgruppe Granit*. Heiner Lange,

for example, was ordered to report to Hildesheim on 9 November for an interview and medical examination. After a brief introduction to the DFS 230 Lange was directed to pilot one of three fully-loaded gliders in a triple tow behind a Ju52. Lange later said the *Fallschirmjäger* were unaware that this was his first flight in the DFS 230. Both the serving and the newly enlisted pilots were trained as infantrymen so they could join the assault groups. Koch ensured this training was thorough as the 42 glider pilots represented 10% of his force.

Much of the flight training took place at night, a new experience for all of the pilots. Kiess was reportedly sceptical that the gliders could be towed successfully at night. Shrouded lights were fitted to the tailplanes of the Ju52s to enable the glider pilots to keep the correct position behind the tugs. Watching some of the gliders conduct a dawn landing on fields wet with dew, Koch again expressed his concern to the pilots about their ability to land in a short distance atop Eben-Emael. To reduce the length of the landing run barbed wire was wrapped around the DFS 230's central skid. Although an improvement it was still not enough. Lange suggested that a brake be fitted that would dig into the ground upon

Above: **Designed in the mid-1930s by Ing. Hans Jacobs, an engineer with the** *Deutsche Forschungsanstalt für Segelflug* **(DFS), the German Gliding Research Institute) the DFS 230 was first flown in early 1937 by** *Flugkapitän* **Hanna Reitsch, a famous female test pilot.** *(PJ)*

Above: **A Ju52 'workhorse' of the *Luftwaffe*. Designed in the late 1920s and first flown in 1932. The all-metal aircraft served with civil airlines before and after World War Two. In *Luftwaffe* service it was used briefly as a bomber, then mainly as a transport. The Ju52 was used in Spain by the *Legion Kondor* and also in countries attacked and occupied by Germany.** *(PJ)*

landing and Koch telephoned the DFS staff to discuss the proposal. Hans Jacobs immediately designed and built a braking device that was fitted to a glider for testing the following day. Internationally-renowned test pilot Hanna Reitsch, who held the world record for the longest flight by a female pilot, padded the glider's control column for protection in the event of an abrupt stop. In spite of this precaution she was dazed when the sudden halt threw her violently against the pilot's harness. Jacobs continued to modify the brake and Reitsch to test it with both empty and fully loaded gliders until they were both satisfied that it would work.

The meticulous planning and preparation which laid the foundation for the success of the operation against Eben-Emael was only possible because Hitler decided to postpone the offensive against France from the proposed date of 12 November. Hitler ordered his commanders on 3 November to plan the capture of Denmark and Norway. The *Fallschirmjäger* of *Sturmabteilung Koch* enviously followed reports of their comrades from I/FJR 1 spearheading the surprise attack on the unprepared Scandinavian countries on 9 April. Their turn would come one month later.

STURMGRUPPE GRANIT – 10 MAY 1940

Glider 1/ *1 Trupp*
Objective 18 (Casemate *Maastricht 2*)
  Leutnant Egon Delica
  Feldwebel Hans Nidermeier
  Feldwebel Gerhard Raschke (pilot)

Richard Drucks	Ludwig Gräf
Willi Krämer	Heinrich List
Richard Tucke	

Glider 2/ *2 Trupp*
Objective 24 (*Coupole 120*)
  Oberjäger Max Maier**
  Unteroffizier Fritz Bredenbeck (pilot)

Paul Bader*	Hans Comdür
Fritz Gehlich	Gerhard Iskra
Walter Meier*	Wilhelm Ölmann

Glider 3/ *3 Trupp*
Objective 12 (Casemate *Maastricht 1*)
  Oberjäger Peter Arent
  Unteroffizier Alfred Sapper (pilot)

Erwin Franz	Paul Kupsch
Gustav Merz*	Josef Müller
Helmut Stopp	

Glider 4/ *4 Trupp*
Objective 19 (MiNord)
  Oberfeldwebel Helmut Wenzel*
  Unteroffizier Otto Bräutigam (pilot)

Kurt Engelmann	Fritz Florian
Fritz Köhler	Karl Polzin
Edmund Schmidt	Paul Windemuth*

Glider 5/ *5 Trupp*
Objective 29 (MICA),
  Feldwebel Erwin Haug
  Unteroffizier Karl-Heinz Lange* (pilot)

Gerhard Becker	Helmuth Bögle**
Ernst Grechza	Egon Hartmann*
Franz Janowski*	Axel Stützinger

Glider 6/ *6 Trupp*
Objective 14 (false cupola)
  Oberjäger Siegfried Harlos
  Unteroffizier Erwini Zille (pilot)

Richard Bläser	Werner Grams
Franz Grigowski	Walter Kippnick
Franz Lukaschek	Peter Zirwes

Glider 7/ *7 Trupp*
Objective 16 (false cupola)
  Oberjäger Fritz Heinemann
  Unteroffizier Heinz Scheidhauer* (pilot)

Wilhelm Alefs	Wihelm Höpfner*
Robert Michalke*	Harm Mülder
Alois Paßmann*	Wolfgang Schulz

Glider 8/ *8 Trupp*
Objective 31 (*Coupole Nord*)
  Oberjäger Karl Unger**
  Unteroffizier Hans Distelmeier (pilot)

Hannes Else*	Ernst Hierländer
Bruno Hooge*	Kajetan Mayr*
Herbert Plietz	Willie Weinert

Glider 9/ *9 Trupp*
Objective 13 (MiSud)
  Oberjäger Ewald Neuhaus
  Unteroffizier Günther Schulz (pilot)

Adolf Jacob*	Johann Körner
Ernst Schlosser*	Anton Seltmann
Toni Wingers	Hans Braun

RECOGNITION SIGNALS FOR STURMGRUPPE GRANIT

We are here and in action

We are occupying this position

We are breaking into this position

Signal for ammunition resupply

Flare Signals

Green: We are here and the mission is going ahead.

Red: Enemy here, attack.

White: Used by the attack troops for emphasis ie: awaiting ammunition. Or as a signal: We are breaking into this bunker.

Whistling Flare: Team commander or replacement dead or wounded.

Glider 10/ Reserve *Trupp*
Oberjäger Willie Hübel**
Unteroffizier Erwin Kraft (pilot)
Bubi Bansimir   Leopold Gilg (radio)
Werner Gutahn   Hubert Hansing
Kurt Jürgensen*   Paul Kautz (radio)

Glider 11/ Reserve *Trupp*
Oberleutnant Rudolf Witzig
Oberjäger Fritz Schwarz
Unteroffizier Karl Pilz (pilot)
Otto Braun*   Uwe Johnsen
Hans-Peter Krenz   Fritz Kruck**

* wounded during operation
** killed during operation

VITAL ROLES FOR THE LUFTWAFFE

The *Luftwaffe* had three primary roles in *Fall Gelb*: clearing the way for airborne and ground operations by a concentrated attack on airfields in Belgium, Holland and France; transporting the airborne forces to their objectives; and, providing air support for the airborne forces and advancing ground forces throughout the campaign.

Planning for the airborne operations in Belgium and Holland was done by a dedicated headquarters, the *Fliegerführer zur besonderen Verwendung* (Air Command for Special Purposes), under the direction of *Generalmajor* Richard Putzier who would later command the airborne forces after Student was wounded in Holland. General Putzier was subordinate to the headquarters of General Albert Kesselring's *Luftflotte 2* (Air Fleet 2) that was responsible for all *Luftwaffe* operations in support of Army Group B.

Allocated to carry *Sturmabteilung Koch* were 50 DFS230 gliders, 42 Ju52 towing aircraft and four spares, six Ju52s to drop reinforcements by parachute and three He111 to drop supplies. The aircraft took off in three waves: the first consisted of 42 Ju52s towing 42 DFS230s, the second wave comprised the six Ju52s carrying the reinforcements that took off 45 minutes after the first and the third wave consisted of the three He111s that took off five minutes after the second wave.

The Ju52s of *Kampfgeschwader zur besonderen Verwendung 5* (KGrzbV 5, Battle Wing for Special Purposes 5) were divided into four squadrons commanded by *Oberleutnant* Hans-Günter Nevries, *Oberletenant* Walter Steinweg, *Leutnant* Günter Seide and *Leutnant* Hans Schweitzer. Each was assigned to one of four assault groups during the early preparation for the operation to ensure that complete trust and confidence developed between the Ju52 and DFS230 pilots.

DFS230 ASSAULT GLIDER

The 1919 Treaty of Versailles that prohibited Germany from developing powered aircraft spurred a great interest in gliders as a means of introducing young Germans to aviation and maintaining an aircraft research and production base. More than 40,000 Germans had been trained to fly gliders by 1937 and thousands of these men became *Luftwaffe* pilots.

In 1932 the Rhön-Rossitten Gesellschaft company, set up by a group of sport glider pilots in 1925, built the experimental OBS glider for meteorological research. The following year the *Deutsche Forschungsanstalt Für Segelflug* (DFS, German Gliding Research Institute) assumed responsibility for the work. *Generalmajor* Ernst Udet, Germany's highest scoring ace during the First World War and director of the *Luftwaffe's Technische Amt* (Technical Office), realised the military potential of the design and the DFS received a contract to develop an 'assault glider' capable of carrying one pilot and up to nine troops.

Engineer Hans Jacobs designed a high-winged monoplane, designated the DFS230, with a fabric covered rectangular steel frame fuselage and stressed plywood wings. A two-wheel undercarriage was used for take-off and jettisoned in flight. A skid was mounted beneath the fuselage for landing and dive brakes were fitted into the upper wing surface. The passengers sat astride a bench, down the centre of the narrow fuselage, that could be removed to increase cargo space. There was a door on the port side of the fuselage immediately beneath the wing and a hatch in the roof that allowed bulky equipment to be loaded. A quick escape could also be made through 'kick out' panels on either side of the fuselage.

Flugkapitän Hanna Reitsch, who in 1931 set the record for the longest glider flight by a female pilot and extended her feat in 1933, flew the first prototype in early 1937 with a Ju52/3m as the towing aircraft. Following a series of trials and demonstrations to senior *Luftwaffe* officers a contract was awarded to Gothaer Waggonfabrik in 1938 for the production of the DFS230A.

The DFS230 was normally towed by a Ju52 but the He111 and later the Ju87 were also used as tow aircraft. The DFS230 had an excellent glide ratio. Released at an altitude of 1,500m (4,921ft) it could glide up to 25km (15.5 miles) in good conditions and a dive speed of 290km/h (180mph) enabled the glider to cover this distance in several minutes. Skilled pilots such as those of *Sturmgruppe Granit* could land the DFS230 within 20m (65.6ft) of a target.

If the DFS230 carried its maximum complement of 10 personnel only 275kg (606lb) of equipment could be carried. Because of the heavy weight of equipment, primarily

Above: **The DFS230 glider as used in the attack on Eben-Emael. Note the opening in the side of the fuselage; this is the 'kick-out' panel which allowed the troop swift egress into combat.** *(PJ)*

demolition charges, needed for the assault on Fort Eben-Emael two of the gliders carried nine personnel, seven gliders carried eight personnel and two carried only seven.

Following combat experience on 10 May 1940 a number of modifications were made to the DFS230 including a braking parachute fitted under the tail and the installation of two fixed forward-firing 7.92mm MG34 machine guns to provide suppressive fire during the glider's landing approach. To provide suppressive fire on the ground a 7.92mm MG15 machine gun could be fitted in an open hatch immediately behind the cockpit that was fired by the first passenger. Gliders with these modifications were given the designation DFS230B-1. Other variants included the DFS230C-1 that had three braking rockets fitted in the nose and was used for the successful 12 September 1943 rescue of Italian dictator Benito Mussolini from house arrest. The larger DFS230F-1, intended to carry up to 15 troops, was designed but never entered production. Estimates of the number of DFS

230s produced in factories in Germany and Czechoslovakia range from 1,569 to a total of over 2,000.

The DFS230 was used for the April 1941 invasion of Greece, the May 1941 airborne assault on Crete, for re-supply missions in North Africa and on the Eastern Front, and for the unsuccessful 25 May 1944 attempt to capture or kill Yugoslavian partisan leader Marshal Tito.

Type:		Assault Glider
Crew:		one
Performance:		
Maximum towing speed:		210km/h (130mph)
Maximum gliding speed:		290km/h (180mph)
Cargo:		
Weights:	Empty:	860kg (1,896lb)
	Loaded:	2,100kg (4,630lb)
Dimensions:		
Wingspan:		21.98m (72ft 1 1/3in)
Length:		11.24m (36ft 10 1/2in)
Height:		2.74m (8ft 11 3/4in)

JUNKERS JU52

The Junkers Ju52, nicknamed *Tante Ju* (Auntie Ju) and *Eisen Annie* (Iron Annie) was the *Luftwaffe's* primary transport aircraft throughout the World War Two. Designed as a passenger aircraft the single-engine Ju52 prototype first flew on 13 October 1930 and was followed by the prototype trimotor Ju52/3m on 7 March 1932. With an all metal airframe covered by a corrugated metal skin the Ju52 was one of the most advanced designs of its time. In 1934 development was completed in secret of the Ju52/3mg3e bomber and 150 were delivered to the *Luftwaffe* by the end of 1935. After the civil war began in Spain, July 1936 a total of 20 Ju52s were among the aircraft that Hitler immediately despatched to support the Nationalist cause and aircraft were also delivered to the Nationalist air force later that year. The type dropped more than 6,000 tonnes of bombs during the three-year conflict. It also demonstrated its transport capabilities; in one operation the Ju52 ferried 10,000 Moorish troops from Morocco to Spain. As purpose-designed bombers, such as the Dornier Do17 and Heinkel He111, entered *Luftwaffe* service the Ju52 became the backbone of the transport fleet and 547 were in service on 1 September 1939.

For airborne operations the Ju52 was used to tow one DFS230 glider or carry a maximum of 13 paratroopers or 18 airlanding infantry. A *Staffel* (squadron) of 12 aircraft was capable of lifting a 156-strong parachute company.

The Ju52's slow speed made the aircraft vulnerable to both ground fire and fighters; during the five day campaign against Holland in May 1940 around 167 Ju52/3ms were lost. As well as improvements to the aircraft's engines, defensive armament and load carrying capability numerous specialised variants of the Ju52 were developed. The Ju52 could be fitted with floats and skis to increase its versatility. An estimated 4,835 of this type, including about 4,600 for the *Luftwaffe*, were built in Germany before Allied bombing halted production in 1944.

Above: **A superb detailed view of a Ju52 trimotor transport. The builder of the aircraft, Junkers pioneered the all-metal airframe and in particular the use of corrugated aluminium.** *(PJ)*

Type:	Medium Transport
Crew:	two
Performance:	
Maximum speed:	305km/h (190 mph)
Cruising speed:	216km/h (34 mph)
Range:	1,300km (808 miles)
Cargo:	2,000kg (4,409lb) or
	18 equipped troops
Weights: Empty:	5,600kg (12,346lb)
Loaded:	11,030kg (24,317lb)
Dimensions:	
Wing span:	29.25m (95ft 11 ¹/₂in)
Length:	18.9m (62ft)
Height:	4.5m (14ft 9in)

Armament: Could be fitted with one 13mm MG 131 machine gun at the dorsal cockpit and two 7.92mm MG 15 machine guns in the beam widows although if these were manned it reduced the carrying capacity.

Above: **An early model of the much feared Junkers Ju87 Stuka. This dive-bomber was used to devastating effect during the *Blitkrieg* for 'pin point' raids in support of ground forces.** *(PJ)*

JUNKERS JU87 STUKA

The Junkers Ju87 was one of four designs by German aircraft manufacturers tested in early 1936 to meet a *Luftwaffe* requirement for a dive bomber (*Sturzkampfflugzeug* or Stuka). Although Hans Pohlmann's Ju87 design was not as technically advanced as the Heinkel He118 it was selected nevertheless and the first production aircraft were delivered in 1937. Three Ju87A-1s and five improved Ju87B-1s were deployed with Germany's Condor Legion in Spain where they proved highly successful. As the *Luftwaffe's* primary close support aircraft the Ju87 was an important element in the success of Germany's *Blitzkrieg* strategy.

Faced with little or no air opposition during the September 1939 invasion of Poland the *Luftwaffe's* nine Ju87 groups (*Stukagruppen*) wrought devastation on Polish forces. If a pilot began his 80^0 dive attack at 3,353m (11,000ft) he would have about 20 seconds to align his reflector sight on the target before releasing his bombs at 693m (2,275ft). With a terminal velocity of no more than 563km/h (350mph) the Ju87's dive would bottom out at 305m (1,000ft). Experienced pilots were expected to place half of their bombs within 24.4m (80ft) of the target. The psychological effect the aircraft's steep screaming dive had upon enemy troops and civilians was enhanced by the fitting of sirens to the Ju87's undercarriage legs.

Almost 360 Ju87s were ready to participate in the Western offensive on 10 May 1940. Only five were lost during the first few days of the campaign. The Ju87 was a rugged and reliable aircraft capable of accurately delivering its bomb load; however, its slow speed and limited defensive armament made it vulnerable to enemy fighters, as quickly became apparent over Dunkirk and during the Battle of Britain. Latter models of the Ju87 armed with two 37mm cannons proved deadly in the anti-tank role on the Russian front.

Type:	Dive Bomber
Crew:	two
Performance:	
Maximum speed:	390km/h (242mph)
Weights: Empty:	2,750kg (6,080kg)
Loaded:	4,250kg (9,371lb)
Dimensions:	
Wing span:	13.8m (45ft 3½in)
Length:	11.1m (36ft 5in)
Height:	3.9m (12ft 9in)

Armament: One forward-firing MG-17 in each wing a single rearward-firing 7.9mm MG-15 machine gun in the rear cockpit.
Bomb Load: One 500kg (1,100lb) bomb on the belly crutch or a 250kg (550lb) bomb on the belly crutch and four 50kg (110lb) bombs on wing racks.

The careful allocation of pilots and the intensive training was rewarded as the nine gliders all landed within the fort, most only tens of metres from their objectives.

5

10 MAY: GLIDER ASSAULT

On 1 May *Sturmabteilung Koch* moved to an unfinished barracks at Ostheim (Hilden Barracks near Düsseldorf) to await the order to attack. Three days later *Generalleutnant* Student (he was promoted in January 1940) was summoned to the Reichschancellery to be told by Hitler that the offensive would begin on 6 May. However, O Day (the German equivalent of D-Day) was postponed and it was not until 9 May that Student's headquarters received the codeword 'Danzig' that alerted all *Wehrmacht* units that Plan *Gelb* would be launched at 05.35 the following morning. Five minutes earlier *Sturmgruppe Granit* was scheduled to land on its objective.

Early on the evening of 9 May the men of *Sturmabteilung Koch* were driven to two air bases outside Köln; Beton, Eisen and Granit assembled at Köln-Ostheim while Stahl moved to Köln-Butzweilerhof. The gliders had been moved earlier to the airfields in furniture vans to hide their loads. They were assembled and meticulously checked under cover in specially built hangers. As the *Fallschirmjäger* waited nervously in their groups their squad leaders

Left: Coupole 120, the damage from a placed 50kg Hohlladungwaffe has been repaired, to hide evidence of the existence of the hollow-charge weapon. (JSS)

Right: **Loverix mill on the main road into the fort (note the sentry box) was badly damaged by Belgian army shelling, including some from the fort.** *(JSS)*

told them to check their equipment and post any last letters. Activity began to increase. The guards who had been patrolling the base since before the arrival of the mysterious furniture vans disappeared to rejoin their unit and at 20.40 trucks arrived carrying *Luftwaffe* ground crew. Some of the *Fallschirmjäger* scrambled into a line when a mobile canteen arrived to dispense coffee, sausages and potatoes. As they drank their coffee the young soldiers watched as the familiar Ju52s landed one after another and ground crew marshalled each aircraft into position. Shortly after 21.00 the hangar doors were opened and

one DFS230 glider was pushed behind each Ju52, the tow cables connected and the release mechanisms tested. When the gliders were all in position the *Fallschirmjäger* were ordered to emplane. After the glider pilots reported all correct, the men were told to leave the stowed equipment, exit the gliders and then assemble in their platoons. *Obergefreiter* Wilhelm Alefts, a member of *Sturmgruppe Granit*, remembered: 'I learned later that sealed orders had now been opened and our job could be announced. *Leutnant* Witzig read the order to us. "*Sturmgruppe Granit* will go by glider to land

Right: ***Bloc 1**, the main entrance into Fort Eben-Emael.* *(FE-E)*

and take a fort in the Belgians' defence system. Ostheim zero hour is 04.25. You have your assignments! That is all." And that is all he said.'

The platoon sergeants instructed their men to get what rest they could and not to stray from the area of the hangars. The non-commissioned officers distributed Pervitin, a stimulant to prevent drowsiness, and collected the wills the men had been told to prepare earlier. At 03.45 the agonising wait finally ended as the squad leaders assembled and checked their men. Witzig gave the order 'An die Maschinen!' ('To the aircraft!') and the Fallschirmjäger followed their squad leaders to their assigned gliders that were marked by chalkboards illuminated by oil lamps. From 04.25 the Ju-52s took off at 30-second intervals jerking the heavily laden gliders into the air. Ten minutes later the last glider of Granit, piloted by Unteroffizier Karl Pilz, lifted off from carrying Witzig and one of the reserve sections. Witzig wrote after the war that 'the failure of the whole mission could be brought about by heavy losses during take-off, flight, landing, and particularly during the critical period when the airborne force was within range of enemy infantry weapons'. The first hurdle was cleared but Witzig would not be as lucky at the second.

The Ju52s from Ostheim circled to the south of Cologne to gain altitude and then rendezvoused with the aircraft of Sturmgruppe Stahl. The armada flew west toward the first of the searchlights that indicated the flight path to the Dutch border. These were spaced at intervals of no more than 15km and were easily identified as a blackout had been enforced in Germany since the start of the war. The towing aircraft had to climb steadily during the 73km flight to an altitude of 2,600m (8,500ft) before reaching the release point near the Dutch border. The air staff planners had calculated this would take about 32 minutes at airspeed of 140km/h.

Sturmgruppe Granit lost two gliders early in the flight. Witzig's DFS 230 was yanked violently downward as the pilot of the towing aircraft was forced to dive steeply to avoid a collision when another Ju52 flew into his path. Although the glider pilot, Karl Pilz, put his DFS230 into a dive the unexpected strain snapped the towrope. When Pilz said he lacked the altitude necessary to glide to the objective Witzig ordered him to turn

Above: **A rare photograph of a Junkers Ju52 with a DFS assault glider on tow. Eleven of each were used to transport** *Sturmgruppe Granit* **to Eben-Emael.** *(JSS)*

back and land as close to Ostheim as possible. Pilz made a successful landing in an unploughed field several kilometres from Cologne. Several minutes later the glider carrying *Feldwebel* Max Meier's *Trupp 2* was released prematurely at an altitude of 1,500m (4,921ft). Lacking sufficient altitude to glide the remaining 60km to the objective Bredenbeck landed near Düren. Unbeknownst to the remainder of the airborne force *Granit* had lost 20 per cent of its combat power before even leaving Germany.

Helped by a strong tailwind the leading aircraft reached the release point, marked by three searchlights northwest of Aachen, 10 minutes earlier than scheduled. To the surprise of the glider pilots the Ju52 pilots did not give the signal to release. Strong wings meant the air armada was 460m (1,509ft) lower than the planned release altitude. Concerned that the gliders lacked sufficient altitude to reach their objectives the senior Ju52 pilot decided to continue flying into Dutch airspace until he reached 2,600m. Soon after the aircraft crossed the Dutch border antiaircraft guns protecting Maastricht began firing. When the Ju52s reached

the correct altitude they released the DFS230s and continued their flight west into Belgium where they dropped parachute dummies stuffed with firecrackers to confuse the Belgians.

As with other Belgian, and Dutch, units along the border the garrison of Fort Eben-Emael had been alerted hours before *Sturmabteilung Koch* had taken off. At 01.30 (00.30 Belgian time) a telephone call from Liège ordered the sergeant of the guard at Eben-Emael to alert the garrison as German troop movements were reported across the border. Although sceptical, as this was the third alert within the past month, the sergeant sounded the alarm claxons and the duty officer telephoned Major Jottrand at his quarters in Eben-Emael village. Jottrand arrived at his command post a short time later and telephoned Liège but received little additional information. Jottrand decided not to order the demolition of the Kanne bridge, the Lanaye lock or to pull down the barracks next to the fort as was stipulated in the standing orders in the event of war. He reasoned that if the long feared invasion had indeed begun he would have adequate time to implement these measures as German ground forces advanced across the Maastricht Appendix.

The soldiers who had been asleep in the two wooden barracks or the village either went straight to their posts or assembled in their teams in the bottom level gallery. Many of the gun crews had hundreds of metres to march through the tunnels to reach their positions and much then needed to be done to prepare the guns for firing such as removing rust-preventing cosmoline and bringing ammunition up from the magazines. The crew of *Coupole Nord* had 640m to move to their position on the east side of the fort as well as two sets of stairs between levels. Despite this, Eben-Emael's standing orders stipulated that *Coupole Nord* would fire an alarm sequence of 20 blank rounds at 30-second intervals to summon garrison members billeted outside the fort. Once aroused and assembled it would take the Wonck detachment more than an hour to march to the fort.

Two hours after Liège had telephoned the alert the warning sequence had not been fired as the crew of *Coupole Nord* was still not at their post. An exasperated Jottrand ordered *Coupole Sud*, where the chief had earlier reported his crew

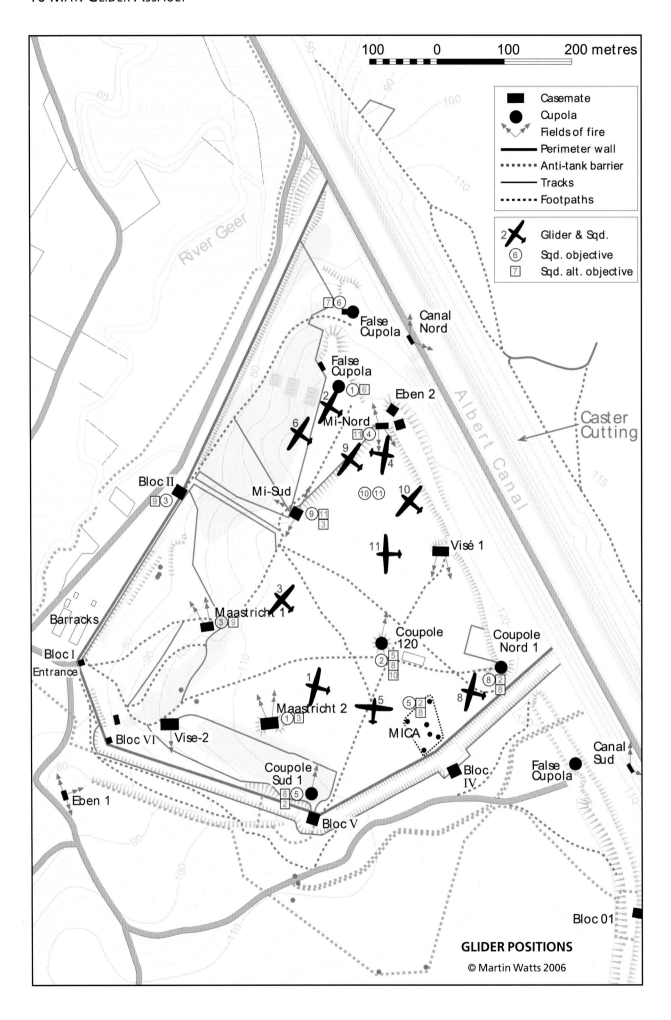

GLIDER POSITIONS

© Martin Watts 2006

Above: **At left is the observation cupola on top of** *Mi-Sud.* **Two DFS 230 gliders are visible and in the background is** *Mi-Nord. (JSS)*

ready, to fire the signal. However, it was almost another hour before *Coupole Sud* fired the alarm sequence as the NCO reported trouble with the ammunition. Finally at 04.25 (03.25) the twin 75mm guns began firing.

Shortly after 05.00 (04.00) Jottrand, then at the entrance block, heard antiaircraft artillery fire from the direction of Maastricht. Convinced this was not a false alarm he ordered the barracks to be destroyed once the stores and other equipment had been moved inside the fort. As the off duty shift had not arrived from Wonck each position was ordered to send a few men to form a work party leaving every position undermanned; the crew of *Coupole Sud* had yet to reach their position.

The reason for the anti-aircraft fire became clearer when a Belgian unit northwest of Kanne reported that from 30 to 50 unidentified aircraft were approaching Belgium from the direction of Maastricht. Shortly afterwards the headquarters of the *2e Grenadier* company at the Kanne bridge reported that aircraft were flying overhead at a high altitude. A curious report was received that aircraft were overhead and that their engines had stopped. One of Jottrand's staff said that the defenders of Vroenhoven bridge had asked for permission to fire on an aircraft landing nearby and that an unidentified voice on the telephone net responded 'Yes!'. Shortly afterwards

machine gun fire was heard from the direction of Vroenhoven bridge; these were the first shots fired by Belgian forces in World War Two. Watching as the strange, silent aircraft descended toward the fort Jottrand realised Eben-Emael was their target. He ordered the Kanne bridge and locks to be blown and directed Captain Alfred Hotermans in the command centre to find out why the anti-aircraft guns were not firing. When told the gunners could not positively identify the aircraft Hotermans shouted into the telephone 'Well, then, shoot! God damn it, shoot!' As the machine guns were mounted for high angle fire it was soon too late. Concerned that there was no explosion from the direction of Kanne Jottrand telephoned the bunker at the bridge and forcefully repeated the order to a sergeant who had been reluctant to execute the order in the absence of the engineer officer who was temporarily away from the post. As their gliders were touching down the men of *Sturmgruppe Eisen* heard the explosion that folded the Kanne bridge into the Albert Canal.

The *Sturmgruppe Granit* pilots were at altitude of about 800m (2,625ft) when Fort Eben-Emael came into view; even in the dawn light they had no difficulty identifying the objective as they followed the Albert Canal south. Putting their gliders into a steep dive they banked right as they passed the fort and then right again

Left:
Fallschirmjäger
after the fall of
Eben-Emael. *(BA)*

toward their individual objectives. In these tense minutes six of the fragile aircraft were hit by fire from the fort's anti-aircraft machine guns but none was seriously damaged. Luck seemed to favour the Germans as two of the Belgian machine guns had jammed. Glider 8 touched down first at 05.24 (04.24) and was followed immediately by Glider 5, piloted by Heiner Lange. So precise was Lange's landing that the DFS230's left wing knocked over two of the anti-aircraft machine guns that were the objective of *Feldwebel* Erwin Haug's squad. Drawing his pistol Lange jumped from the DFS230 cockpit into one of the gun pits where four shocked Belgians raised their hands in surrender. Lange was equally shocked when a grenade thrown by Haug landed in the same pit. Neither the German pilot nor the Belgian gunners were injured as the grenade either failed to detonate properly or the explosion was absorbed by soft ground. Haug's squad charged toward the gun firing in the next pit and a second hand grenade was thrown that killed one of the gun crew and left two others dazed. The anti-aircraft guns were silenced in a few minutes.

The careful allocation of pilots and their intensive training was rewarded as the nine gliders all landed within the fort, most only tens of metres from their objectives. Witzig's

absence was not noticed as the nine squad leaders set about their well rehearsed missions. The task of seven-strong *1 Trupp*, led by *Feldwebel* Hans Nidermeier, was to destroy *Maastricht 2* with its three 75mm guns trained toward the canal bridges. Nidermeier and another *Fallschirmjäger* assembled a 50kg *Hohlladungwaffe* charge on the centre of the observation cupola atop Maastricht 2. The two Belgian sergeants peering through the cupola's small vision blocks apparently did not see the glider land as they only reported seeing the boots of men clambering over the cupola before the charge exploded killing them both. Nidermeier was unable to locate a second 'turret' that intelligence had said was on the casemate. A 12.5kg *Hohlladungwaffe* charge was then exploded beneath one of the three 75mm guns with murderous effect: two Belgian gunners were killed immediately and two others fatally wounded. Some of the survivors dragged wounded men down the stairs out of the shattered casemate. Nidermeier and two others scrambled through the hole and fired several bursts from their MP38/40s down the stairwell. On the level below the Belgians shut the steel door, placed the prepositioned steel beams in their slots and stacked the filled sandbags before shutting the second door. The *Fallschirmjäger*

Right: **Men of *Sturmabteilung Koch* (Assault Group Koch) after the glider attacks of 10 May 1940. Group Koch had a complement of 11 officers and 427 other ranks which included 42 glider pilots.** *(BA)*

laid out a recognition panel on the cupola to indicate to the Ju87s that the position was in German hands.

The mission of the missing *2 Trupp* was to destroy *Coupole 120* and it would be sometime before the squad's absence was noticed. After its glider landed less than 30m from *Maastricht 1 Feldwebel* Peter Arent's *3 Trupp* quickly silenced the threat to the canal bridges posed by the casemate. After fruitlessly searching for an infantry exit from which intelligence analysts had warned the Belgians could launch a counterattack, the squad exploded a 12.5kg *Hohlladungwaffe* charge beneath one of the three 75mm guns. The explosion hurtled the gun across the casemate, killing one of the gunners in its path before plunging down the stairwell. The Germans sprayed fire into the gaping hole before three *Fallschirmjäger* climbed into the smoking interior. Hearing voices at the bottom of the stairwell Arent dropped a 3kg conventional charge down the shaft. Taking a dazed prisoner with him the NCO climbed down the stair to find the steel door at the bottom had been barricaded.

The first objective of *Hauptfeldwebel* Helmut Wenzel's *4 Trupp* was to destroy *Mi Nord*, one of the two machine gun emplacements that provided close defence of the fort's superstructure. Wenzel sprinted 100m from where his glider landed to the wall of the casemate where found the gun embrasures closed. Scrambling up the grassy side slope he shoved a 1kg charge through the periscope opening. When the machine guns began firing Wenzel exploded a 50kg *Hohlladungwaffe* charge on the centre of the observation cupola. Although the charge did not penetrate the 15.24cm (6in) armour it knocked the cupola out of the ring mount and the bunker's stunned occupants retreated down the stairs. Not satisfied with the results of the first charge Wenzel exploded another near a gun embrasure that smashed through the casemate's concrete wall leaving the steel reinforcing rods exposed. Using his torch Wenzel climbed inside and picked up a telephone that rang soon afterwards. Unable to understand the speaker Wenzel initially responded in German before stating slowly 'Here are the Germans'. After a short pause the voice exclaimed '*Mon Dieu!*' and the line went dead. Leaving the bunker Wenzel ordered the squad to establish platoon headquarters and, after sending some runners to find Witzig, set off to check the progress of the other squads. He encountered one of the platoon's signallers, who arrived with Glider 10, and was also looking for Witzig. Wenzel directed him to platoon headquarters and sent the first situation report to Koch: 'From *Sturmgruppe*

Granit, reached objective, everything going to plan.'

After silencing the anti-aircraft emplacement, Haug led *Trupp 5* to attack *Coupole Sud* situated on a rocky promontory above *Bloc V* at the south of the fort. After exploding a demolition charge on the cupola while it was retracted the squad them moved along the top of the wall toward *Bloc IV*. Although the explosion damaged one of the two 75mm guns the Belgian crew soon had the weapon in operation, although at a reduced rate of fire. Repeated attacks by Ju87s proved unsuccessful and the cupola remained a significant threat both to *Granit* and advancing German ground forces until the fort was surrendered.

The failure of German intelligence to detect the two false cupolas toward the northern tip of Eben-Emael meant that the efforts of two squads, 6 and 7, were wasted attacking these dummy positions during the crucial initial stage of the operation.

Feldwebel Karl Unger's squad in Glider 8 had come to a stop about 30m (33ft) from *Coupole Nord*. As the squad ran toward the cupola one *Fallschirmjäger* was hit by small arms fire from a building near *Coupole 120* behind them. The building was not part of Eben-Emael's defences but a maintenance facility in which tools were stored. Three men were detailed to deal with this threat while Unger and two other sappers first detonated a 50kg *Hohlladungwaffe* charge and then a 12.5kg *Hohlladungwaffe* charge against the steel emergency exit on the side of the casemate. The second charge blew the door off its hinges and collapsed the concrete above thus sealing the exit. Although the Belgian crew had seen the gliders land they were slow bringing up the 75mm ammunition from the magazine below. When the ammunition hoist failed to function one NCO carried several rounds up the stairs and the crew frantically loaded the twin guns. Before the Belgians could fire their first shell another 50kg *Hohlladungwaffe* charge exploded atop the cupola killing and wounding crew members, wrenching the guns from their mounts and damaging the mechanism that raised, lowered

Above: **The flat area on top of the fortress where the gliders of *Sturmgruppe Granit* landed. This 1940 photograph was taken from *Maastricht 2* and shows *Coupole 120,* to the left is *Visé I* in the background.** *(JSS)*

Above Right: **One of the many air vents around Fort Eben-Emael which supplied fresh air into the tunnels.** *(JSS)*

Right: **A** *Fallschirmjäger* **with a 27mm Walther** *Leuch-pistole* **(flare pistol).** *(BA)*

and traversed the cupola. A machine gun that was firing from an embrasure was silenced by a small demolition charge. Artillery fire, possibly from the still *Coupole Sud*, began exploding around *Coupole Nord* killing Unger. At 05.45 the survivors within *Coupole Nord* received an order from Jottrand to abandon their position and seal the entrance doors in the tunnel below.

As Unger was leading the attack on the primary objective his MG34 gunner remained near the glider to provide covering fire as two other *Fallschirmjäger* approached the building and detonated a 3kg charge against a door. After the explosion firing from the building ceased.

The DFS230 carrying *Feldwebel* Ewald Neuhaus' *9 Trupp* came to a halt in a barbed wire entanglement 55m (60yd) from *Mi Sud*, the second machine gun emplacement that covered Eben-Emael's superstructure. Although the glider had been hit by anti-aircraft fire over Maastricht and by machine gun fire from Eben-Emael none of the squad was injured. The men crawled through a gap that Neuhaus cut through

the wire. One of the sappers tried to jam a 12.5kg *Hohlladungwaffe* charge between one of the machine guns and the top of the embrasure but the Belgian defenders used a cleaning rod to push the charge off before it exploded. While sappers threw grenades through the embrasures others placed a 50kg *Hohlladungwaffe* that blew in a steel door giving them an entrance to the bunker. The stunned Belgians offered no further resistance. After positioning an MG34 gunner at an embrasure covering toward the west and placing the rest of the squad in positions outside Neuhaus sent a runner to report to Witzig.

With Witzig's glider nowhere to be seen Wenzel took charge of the assault force. Although *Leutnant* Egon Delica, who had landed in Glider 1, was nominally second-in-command he was a communications specialist whose primary task was to coordinate air support from the Ju87s. After the war Wenzel said that 'the officers had trained all of the men so well that the officers were expendable'.

Jottrand listened with mixed emotions to the fragmentary reports he received from the survivors that made their way to his command post 40m below the surface. At 05.50 (04.50) headquarters of the RFL in Liège logged a message from Eben-Emael that 30 Germans had landed on top of the fort. Within 10 minutes Colonel Modard, RFL commander, directed the 150mm guns of Fort Barchon and Fort Pontisse to bombard Eben-Emael. Jottrand organised six patrols or counter-attacks on the superstructure over the next 24 hours. However, the combination of no infantry training, few automatic weapons, the difficulty of coordinating supporting artillery fire and the lack of aggressive spirit doomed each of these efforts. Shortly after 06.00 (05.00) a patrol of 12 volunteers edged along the antitank ditch to *Bloc IV* where they witnessed the explosion of a *Hohlladungwaffe*. Attacked by Ju87s the patrol returned to report to Jottrand that the Germans were using a very large calibre howitzer.

At about 06.35 (05.35) Ju87 dive bombers and Henschel Hs126 reconnaissance aircraft circled the fort. The aircraft were unable to establish radio contact with *Granit* but observed that panels in the shape of a swastika were spread out on most of the fort's

emplacements. The aircraft bombed the entrance to the fort at *Bloc 1*, the barracks and the village of Eben-Emael killing 36 civilians and wounding many more. The fatalities included the wife and two children of Sergeant Lecron who lived in a house less than 100m (109yd) from the fort's entrance. Allowed to leave the fort Lecron rescued his infant daughter from the wreckage of his home and returned to the comparative safety of the fort.

Jottrand sent officers along the tunnels to report on the situation. One officer sent to MiN went no further than the barricaded entrance before returning; an angry Jottrand ordered him to repeat the 40-minute trip to make a more thorough reconnaissance. Wearing gas masks the fort's chaplain and another officer felt their way along the smoke and dust filled tunnels to *Maastricht 1* and began climbing the stairs.

*Above: **Bloc I**, the entrance to the fort, photographed in March 1941 from the direction of **Bloc IV**. The bombed-out remains of the barracks are in the background. Note the anti-tank 'hedgehog' type defences held in line by heavy steel cables. (JSS)*

*Right: A Henschel **HS 126** observation aircraft in service in Russia. The same type was used for target-spotting for Ju87 Stukas in the attack on Eben-Emael. (PJ)*

After surviving the explosion of a demolition charge dropped by the Germans down the shaft the shaken officers scrambled back and with much effort closed both doors isolating the casemate. As the reports built up Jottrand decided it would be impossible to recapture the lost emplacements from the intermediate level. He ordered barricades built in the Level 1 tunnels in the event the Germans succeeded in rupturing any of the steel doors; 18 barricades were built.

Above: **Observation cupola *Eban 2* on top of *Mi-Nord*.** *(FE-E)*

*Left: **Mi-Nord** shows the effect of exploding a 50kg Hohlladung-waffe against the wall of the emplacement. The attack was by 4 Trupp led by Oberfeldwebel Helmut Wenzel.* *(FE-E)*

Above: **Coupole 120** after the attack. An armoured cover has been refitted over one of the gun slits. Damage from a *Hohlladungwaffe* can be seen above the nearest gun. *(JSS)*

Right: **Mi-Sud** was 'knocked-out' by **9 Trupp** led by *Feldwebel* Neuhaus using a 50kg *Hohlladung-waffe* hollow-charge weapon and hand grenades. *(PJ)*

To Jottrand's frustration the heavy guns of *Coupole 120* had yet to fire. Only the previous day the crew had rehearsed its gun drills with no difficulty but on the morning of 10 May vital tools were missing and the ammunition lift would not function. Later speculation blamed sabotage but no proof has ever been found. One of the crew fired his rifle through the sight aperture killing a *Fallschirmjäger* and also wounding one of

the Belgian prisoners that he was guarding. Lange was marshalling Belgian prisoners from the anti-aircraft battery past the cupola toward platoon headquarters when an exploding shell peppered him with shrapnel. Observing that *Coupole 120* was rotating Lange returned to his glider and despite his wounds struggled back with both sections of a 50kg *Hohlladungwaffe* that he exploded on the armoured dome. Hampered by his injuries Lange was unable to reach shelter and the explosion deafened him for life. Nevertheless Lange was able to protect the prisoners when a member of his squad, Ernst Grechza, appeared and threatened to shoot the Belgians. The night before Grechza had filled his water bottle with rum thinking it would be useful if anyone was wounded but in the tension he had gulped it himself. The intoxicated sapper straddled one of the 120mm barrels and held on as the turret continued to rotate. An angry Wenzel arrived and ordered Grechza off the gun and then dropped 3kg charges down each barrel. Dazed by the explosions the Belgian crew

abandoned *Coupole 120* and barricaded the entrance on the intermediate level.

The second task assigned to the missing *2 Trupp* was to put Casemate *Visé 1* out of action. Wenzel directed *Feldwebel* Willie Hübel's *10 Trupp*, one of the two reserve squads, to destroy the casemate which was less than 40m (14.5yd) from where his squad was sheltering. Over the previous six months Hübel had studied and rehearsed the tasks of each of the assault squads. Within five minutes of receiving Wenzel's order Hübel detonated a 12.5kg *Hohlladungwaffe* atop *Visé 1*, knocking out another of Eben-Emael's offensive gun emplacements.

After Wenzel established radio contact with Koch two He111 bombers flew over Eben-Emael at an altitude of about 180m (590ft) and dropped supply containers with additional ammunition and water. Not wishing to expose his own men Wenzel ordered the Belgian prisoners who were sheltering near *Mi Nord* to collect the canisters. Shortly afterwards the *Fallschirmjäger* watched with curiosity as a lone

Above: **The devastating effect of exploding a 50kg hollow-charge weapon against reinforced concrete.** *(FE-E)*

Right: German troops of the occupying force examine *Mi-Nord* and Observation Cupola *Eben 2* mounted on top of the emplacement. *(FE-E)*

DFS230 appeared from the east and glided to a landing near *Mi Nord*. To the surprise and delight of his men Witzig climbed out of the glider and ran toward his platoon sergeant. 'It was a testament to Witzig's personality that he was able to get back to the fight,' said Wenzel in a postwar interview. After inspecting the DFS230 and the field where he had landed Pilz assured Witzig that he would be able to take off. Witzig directed *Trupp 11* to clear any obstructions and then ran to a nearby village where he found a military garrison. The determined paratrooper convinced an officer of his identity and was given a car to drive to Ostheim. The airfield's operations office located an available Ju52 at Goetersich that soon collected Witzig and then located the glider. The transport pilot had the foresight to bring a tow cable and DFS230 landing gear that the squad fitted to the glider with the aid of a few civilians.

Witzig was no doubt satisfied when Wenzel briefed him on the situation. Acting initially as individual squads and later under Wenzel's

aggressive direction the nine squads that reached Eben-Emael had completed the first phase of *Granit's* mission. They had knocked out the anti-aircraft battery, both of the defensive machine gun casemates and the heavy guns threatening the bridges over the Albert Canal. To this point the force had suffered two dead and about a dozen wounded. Witzig directed the second phase, holding the position until ground forces arrived to complete the capture of the fort. The plan called for the relief force to arrive at Eben-Emael five hours after crossing the Dutch border. Neither Koch nor Witzig were aware that the timetable for their relief was meaningless as Dutch forces delayed the German advance across the Maastricht Appendix by almost a day by destroying bridges across the Maas. As Belgian artillery fire landed on Eben-Emael Witzig was certain that it was the prelude to a counterattack by a Belgian force that would heavily outnumber his own paratroopers.

The counterattacks that Witzig feared were ill conceived and poorly executed. At 09.00

(08.00) another 12-strong patrol from the fort retraced the route of the first patrol but when they saw unidentified troops moving from the southwest towards the fort's entrance they quickly returned to *Bloc 1* fearing that they would be cut off. The approaching troops were a 40-strong platoon from the *4e Bataillon 2e Regiment de Grenadiers* that had been ordered at 09.30 (08.30) to stage a counterattack. Anticipating that the seizure of the canal bridges was the prelude to a major attack, *2e Grenadiers* headquarters had decided that a platoon would be adequate to clear Eben-Emael of 30 Germans. After completing a march of 4.5km in only an hour the grenadiers were shocked when they found Eben-Emael village in ruins. Unfamiliar with the fort's layout Lt Wagemans led his platoon to the fort's entrance to seek assistance and Jottrand provided two officers to guide the platoon to retake *Maastricht 1* and *Maastricht 2*. A bomb from a Ju87 killed a grenadier and wounded two others before the platoon moved into the trees on the northwest side of the fort. The attention of the Ju87s and Belgian artillery fire prevented the small force from launching a determined concerted counterattack. Until 20.30 (19.30) they remained under the cover of the trees exchanging fire with any of Witzig's men who appeared near *Maastricht 1*, *Maastricht 2* and *Visé 1*. His ammunition exhausted, and refused entry to the fort by Jottrand in accordance with Eben-Emael's standing orders, Wagemans led his platoon back to its original position at Loen.

During the daylight hours of 10 May the guns of Fort Pontisse fired 1,000 rounds of 105mm on Eben-Emael, Fort Barchon fired 250 rounds of 150mm and Fort Evegnee another 40 rounds of 150mm ammunition. With no accurate observation on Eben-Emael's superstructure this fire possibly did as much to disrupt the coordination of Belgian counter-attacks as harm the men of *Granit*, many of whom sheltered in the ruptured cupolas and casemates.

The two casemates at the base of the canal and the detached *Bloc 01* offered effective resistance to the main German advance. At about 11.00 (10.00) Belgian observers in observation cupola Eben 1, on the roof of *Bloc 01*, saw German engineers in the Dutch village of Eysden begin building a pontoon bridge. Dutch troops had blown up the road bridge across the Meuse before the Germans could capture it. The observers directed the fire of the 75mm guns of *Coupole Sud* on the crossing site. Target information was relayed to Forts Barchon and Pontisse that later joined the bombardment. The Belgian fire disrupted the German bridge building efforts, killing 21 soldiers and a number of Dutch civilians as well as heavily damaging the village. Stukas targeted *Bloc 01* throughout the day; although their bombs did not destroy the casemate the dust and smoke they caused would sometimes limit observation.

The 60mm anti-tank gun at *Canal Nord* fired whenever Germans tried to cross the collapsed bridge at Kanne. The 75mm guns of *Canal Sud* and *Visé 2* shelled Lanaye whenever German

Below: **The entrance to *Coupole Nord* which was attacked by *Trupp 8* under the command of Feldwebel Karl Unger. The door was blown in by a single 50kg *Hohlladungwaffe*. A second 12.5kg charge collapsed the concrete roof thus sealing the doorway.** *(FE-E)*

Right: **A soldier exits the hole left by a 50kg** *Hohlladungwaffe* **charge and gives scale to the effect of this weapon.** *(FE-E)*

Below: **Bloc-1, the entrance to the fort was attacked by** *Pionier-bataillon 51* **using anti-tank guns.** *(FE-E)*

activity was seen in the area. *Feldwebel* Nidermeier made two attempts during the afternoon to destroy *Coupole Sud*. The first was abandoned when a flight of Ju87s bombed the cupola and the second when Nidermeier decided there was too much small arms fire to successfully approach the armoured dome.

In the early afternoon Jottrand, convinced that only a counterattack in strength would succeed, ordered Lieutenant Edgar Levaque to move the 233-strong relief shift from Wonck to Eben-Emael's aid. The column was attacked by Ju87s almost soon at it began its march. After more than two hours Levaque and about a dozen men reached the fort; over the coming hours another 85 or so men succeeded in reaching Eben-Emael. Their accounts of constant air attack only served to further undermine the morale of the garrison. Nevertheless at 18.45 (17.45) about 100 volunteers left the fort to make another attempt on *Maastricht 1*. Met by German small arms fire and pounded by Stukas the Belgians withdrew into the fort after less than an hour. Another attempt by 60 volunteers was thwarted when Ju87s bombed the entrance *Bloc I*. Ordered to

leave through the exit in *Bloc II* the Belgians were met by a tremendous shock wave as they moved through the tunnel when Witzig's men exploded a *Hohlladungwaffe* against the *Bloc II* exit. Anticipating that that Germans would try to force an entrance into the fort the Belgians built and manned a sandbag barrier blocking the tunnel to *Bloc II*.

However, Witzig's intention was not to penetrate the fort but to deter a Belgian counterattack from within Eben-Emael and neutralise the threat to advancing German ground forces from *Canal Nord* and *Bloc II*. *Trupp 6*, led by *Oberjäger* Siegfried Harlos, was given the difficult task of attacking *Canal Nord*. Harlos used rope to lower a *Hohlladungwaffe* alongside the casemate and detonated the charge using primer cord. Three attempts were made with no perceptible effect. Fire from German ground forces on the east side of the canal proved no more successful and the casemate remained in action until the surrender of the fort.

To deter German activity during the night Jottrand ordered the emplacements that were still operable to fire periodically. *Coupole Sud*

Above: **German engineers repair damage to a bridge over the Maas (Meuse) River. The photograph clearly shows the inflatable boats used by German forces for this purpose and also for assault.** *(JSS)*

Above: **Bridge destroyed by Belgian forces. Troops are being ferried across the Albert Canal in inflatable boats. Later, German engineers constructed a temporary bridge alongside the original.** *(JSS)*

continued to periodically sweep across the superstructure with anti-personnel shells. Jottrand also requested fire missions from Fort Pontisse which fired a further 750 rounds of 105mm and 200 rounds of 75mm ammunition at Eben-Emael during the night of 10-11 May.

Colonel Walter Melzer's *Infanterie-Regiment 151*, with *Oberstleutnant* Hans Mikosch's *Pionierbataillon 51* (PiBtl51) under command spearheaded the German advance toward Eben-Emael. Mikosch's mission was to relieve Witzig and complete the capture of the fort. The destruction of the bridges in Maastricht slowed the German advance until an assault bridge was erected across the Maas (Meuse). By late afternoon the lead elements of PiBtl 51 reached Kanne. The demolition of the Kanne bridge further slowed the relief force as this was the designated route for the combat engineers. *Oberfeldwebel* Josef Portsteffen's platoon was detached from the battalion and ordered to cross the Albert Canal in line with the northern tip of Fort Eben-Emael to make contact with Witzig's force as quickly as possible. Repeated attempts by Porsteffen's sappers to cross the canal in assault boats

during the last hours of daylight were driven back by fire from *Canal Nord*. Under cover of darkness they tried again at about 23.00 (22.00) and succeeded in crossing the canal despite coming under intense fire. Portsteffen's platoon cautiously made its way along the canal until the junction with the moat at the fort's northern tip and then followed the moat until they reached the area of *Bloc II* about dawn. Portsteffen began his assault on *Bloc II* using a flamethrower and followed this with a 50kg conventional charge. The noise and smoke caused the Belgian sergeant commanding the detachment at the sandbag barrier blocking the tunnel to *Bloc II* to erroneously report that the Germans had blown the steel doors. The platoon moved on *Mi Sud* where they dropped explosives down the shaft which the blew the doors and the steel barrier off their supports. The Belgians soon abandoned the barricades in the tunnels to both positions. Witzig and Portsteffen agreed to keep the pressure on the garrison until Mikosch's battalion arrived. Knowing that relief was not far off several of the *Fallschirmjäger* were keen to use up the last of their explosives. Sappers from the two units

dropped charges through the embrasures or down the shafts of several emplacements. Daylight brought no boost for Eben-Emael's defenders; some of those in the casemates were afraid to open the embrasures for fear of attracting a German grenade or demolition charge. The tunnels and rooms in the smoke and dusk filled interior of the fort were now only lit by lamps or torches. Chlorine fumes made the atmosphere even more stifling.

North of the demolished Kanne bridge Mikosch had worked through the night ferrying his men and dismantled equipment across the canal in assault boats.

By dawn he had positioned anti-tank guns in Eben-Emael village where they could fire on *Bloc I* and the nearby *Bloc VI* from a range of a few hundred metres. At around 09.00 (08.00) these guns began firing on *Bloc I* forcing Jottrand to abandon his intention of staging another counterattack. Later in the morning German antitank guns and machine guns were in position to fire on *Bloc IV*. The casemate was untouched during the *Fallschirmjäger* assault and its frustrated crew were glad to finally have

a target to engage. Both 60mm guns were soon put out of action by high-velocity anti-tank shells. After the crew exhausted their machine gun ammunition Jottrand ordered the casemate abandoned and the tunnel sealed. After inspecting *Maastricht 1* and *Maastricht 2* Jottrand divided the headquarters staff – several were left to man the fire direction centre while the remainder were ordered to set up a command post on Level 0. At 09.45 (08.45) Jottrand briefed his superior headquarters that Eben-Emael's situation was desperate: the attackers on the fort's superstructure had been joined by forces outside the fort, only a few emplacements were operable, 25 of the garrison were dead and 63 wounded. He urged a counterattack from outside the fort. The commander of the III Army Corps in Liège, his artillery commander and the commander of I Army Corps discussed Eben-Emael's plight. No one was willing to order the fort's surrender. III Army Corps sought guidance from General Headquarters where a junior staff drafted a reply: 'Alone, only the commander of the fort can decide if it should cease its defence.

Above: **A view of the Caster cut (Albert Canal) from** *Coupole Nord.* **Note the anti-infantry barbed-wire on the side of the emplacement.** *(F-E-E)*

Above right: **One of the many bridges over the Maas (Meuse) destroyed before and during the** *Blitzkrieg* **on 10 May 1940. Weirs and locks which controlled the level of water were also destroyed by the defenders.** *(JSS)*

Right: **The remains of Kanne bridge over the Albert Canal, destroyed by Belgian forces.** *(JSS)*

He must consult his defence council. If there is a surrender the commander of the fort must blow up the works after it has been evacuated by its defenders. If the evacuation of the garrison is impossible, you are ordered to blow up the fort and all its men.' After receiving this message Jottrand held a council of war at which his officers unanimously urged him to surrender. Hoping to rally his men in the tunnels for a breakout attempt, Jottrand's voice was drowned by others demanding he surrender.

Jottrand ordered Captain Vamecq to negotiate a surrender as he set about supervising the destruction of the fort's remaining guns and classified papers. The crew chief destroyed the twin 75mm guns in *Coupole Sud* by firing them while the cupola was retracted. A charge placed in *Visé 2* failed to explode leaving its guns intact. The last defender to be killed was a soldier who volunteered to ignite the explosives that were prepositioned to close the tunnel to the detached *Bloc 01* after its crew had withdrawn. He was killed in the explosion although

it was never determined whether this was by choice or by accident.

At about 13.15 (12.15) the Germans, including the lead companies of Infantry Regiment 151 which had arrived about one hour earlier, heard a bugle call and saw a white flag appear from the fort's entrance. Vamecq was met by a German officer but before the negotiations began hundreds of demoralised Belgian soldiers began filing out of the fort. Jottrand was the last to leave the fort after the wounded had been carried out. In response to *Oberstleutnant* Mikosch, Jottrand gave an assurance that his men had left no delayed mines in the fort.

Witzig's force buried their six dead comrades, including *Oberjäger* Max Maier who had been killed in Kanne, within the fort and then moved into Eben-Emael village where they found a tavern. As the jubilant *Fallschirmjäger* drank Belgian beer they watched the fort's garrison march past to begin five years of captivity. Among the last was Sergeant Lecron carrying his daughter on his

Above: **Casemate Visé I**, was attacked in the absence of **2 Trupp** by **10 Trupp** commanded by **Feldwebel** Willie Hübel. A 12.5kg **Hohlladungwaffe** was exploded on the top of this casemate thus putting it out of action. *(FE-E)*

Above: **A damaged house in Eben-Emael village with a sign for the direction to the fort.** *(FE-E)*

shoulders. At the insistence of a German officer the girl was left in a convent in Maastricht where her grandfather located her two years later. *Sturmgruppe Granit*, carrying those of the 20 wounded who could not walk, then marched slowly to Kanne and on to Maastricht where they spent the night sleeping on the floor of a school. *Sturmgruppe Granit* received a tumultuous reception when it was driven into Ostheim that evening. The following day the group continued to Munster where General Kesselring awarded the Iron Cross 1st Class to every enlisted member and each was promoted one rank with the exception of Grechza who received a 2nd Class medal and no promotion. Following six months of virtual isolation that culminated with 30 hours of combat at Eben-Emael the *Fallschirmjäger* were given a 14-day leave.

2 TRUPP'S WAR

Despite landing in a field near Düren *Oberjäger* Max Maier was determined that the eight-strong *2 Trupp* was not going to miss the

operation. After commandeering a passing motorcycle he succeeded in borrowing two staff cars from an engineer unit. Threading their way through the long columns of men and vehicles moving across the Maastricht Appendix he reached Kanne in the late morning only to discover the bridge blown. Seeing *Sturmgruppe Eisen* engaged in a firefight on the west side of the canal the determined NCO was crawling across the bridge's superstructure when he was mortally wounded by small arms fire. Undeterred, the squad's second-in-command *Gefreiter* Walter Meier succeeded in crossing the bridge, found a bicycle and pedalled to the village of Eben-Emael. He removed a copy of the fort's daily orders from a notice board outside the wooden barracks as proof that he had reached the fort and returned to Kanne to collect his squad. After being wounded crossing the bridge Meier was unable to locate his squad who were trading fire with Belgians on both sides of the canal. One squad member marched 121 Belgians to a prisoner-of-war collection point.

Left: **The heavy damage to Eben-Emael village was not only from air attack but from shells fired into the fort with fire directed from three other Belgian forts.** *(FE-E)*

Below: **The spire of Eben-Emael church stands above the heavily damaged village.** *(FE-E)*

Above **A Belgian T-13 light tank used to counter-attack at Vroenhoven but two were immobilised by fire from** *Panzerbüsche 38/39* **weapons. This T-13 carries temporary German markings.** *(TM)*

Right: **One of the many bridges over the Maas (Meuse) destroyed by the defenders to slow the German advance.** *(JSS)*

TWO BRIDGES CAPTURED INTACT

The first gliders to land on 10 May were those of *Sturmgruppe Beton* which touched down under fire near the western end of the Vroenhoven bridge at 05.15. One of the group's gliders had been forced to land at Hottdorf, Germany after its towrope broke. Fire from the defending company of the *18e Régiment d'Infanterie de Ligne* damaged the controls of a DFS230 causing it to crash from an altitude of about 10m (33ft) injuring three of the occupants. The defensive positions on the three objective bridges were sited to cover an attack from the east not from the Belgian side of the canal. One of *Leutnant* Schacht's *Fallschirmjäger* stormed through the open door of a bunker in time to cut the fuse of the demolition charge that was lit only moments before. Thus *Beton* secured its objective within 10 minutes of landing. As Schacht's glider landed more than a kilometre from the objective the critical task of organising the defence of the bridge was undertaken by his platoon sergeant. Three squads were positioned

at each end of the bridge. The 24-strong detachment of reinforcements arrived on schedule although one man was killed by ground fire and another drowned in the canal. Later in the day *Beton* beat off at least one counter-attack. Schacht was relieved by the leading elements of *4.Panzer-Division* at 21.40. *Sturmgruppe Beton* lost 10 *Fallschirmjäger* killed and 29 wounded.

Having quickly established his headquarters at Vroenhoven bridge Koch's signal detachment received a report from *Leutnant* Altmann at 05.35 that *Sturmgruppe Stahl* had captured Veltwezelt bridge intact although fighting was continuing. Stahl had landed about 15 minutes earlier under small arms fire from the *6e Companie, 2e Regiment de Carabiniers*. One of the glider pilots was wounded causing his DFS230 to plunge into the ground from an altitude of about 10m injuring all but two of the occupants. Altmann's men used a *Hohlladungwaffe* to neutralise a casemate on the western end of the bridge killing the 12

Above and right: **The Dutch demolished Eysden bridge which crossed the Maas (Meuse) up river from Lanaye locks. Here a German artillery unit is crossing the river using a captured lighter. The hill in the background is the Dutch side of the Caster cut. The photographs are dated May 1940.** *(JSS)*

Above: **Troops of the occupying forces at lunch by the entrance to *Bloc-I*. The south wall of the fortress can be seen in the background and in the distance is *Bloc VI*. (FE-E)**

defenders from the *2e Regiment de Cyclistes Frontière*. Another demolition charge jammed the door of a casemate built into the western pile of the bridge to cover the canal; its occupants remained trapped until German sappers opened the door the following day. Within 10 minutes of landing the bridge was in German hands. At 06.15 24 machine gunners parachuted on the west side of the canal; two were killed in the drop and another wounded. That afternoon four T-13 light tanks from the 7 DI's tank company probed the *Fallschirmjäger*'s defences but retired after two were disabled by 7.92mm armour piercing bullets fired from the *Panzerbüchse 38/39* anti-tank attachment to the 98K rifle. Early that evening Altmann's men had the satisfaction of watching the first German tanks cross the Meuse. Eight members of *Stahl* were killed and 30 wounded before responsibility for the bridge was turned over to *4.Panzer-Division* at 21.30.

As at Eben-Emael, Ju87s supported the three assault groups at the bridges throughout the day, hindering the ability of the Belgians to launch a concerted counterattack. One Belgian account described the Ju87s attacking in waves at 30-minute intervals that were reduced to 15 minutes as the day wore on. Stukas bombed and strafing Belgian units in their assembly areas. One strike was particularly crucial. The defence of the bridges at Veltwezelt and Vroenhoven was the responsibility of Commandant Giddeloo headquartered in the village of Lanaeken. Simultaneous with the landing of *Sturmabteilung Koch*, four Ju87s bombed the command post, killing the Belgian commander and 20 other personnel, thus ensuring that in the first minutes of the assault on the two bridges there was no one to order their destruction.

At 05.40 Koch received a disappointing radio report from *Sturmgruppe Eisen* that Kanne bridge was blown, although engineers should be able to bring the bridge back into service. The report also said that opposition was 'rather strong'. Having received no further reports from Eisen either by radio or runner Koch dispatched a patrol about 12.00 to investigate the situation. About two hours

Above: **In the background of this photograph is the main entrance to** *Bloc-1* **and anti-tank defences. To the left are the remains of the barracks destroyed by bombs from Ju 87 Stukas.** *(FE-E)*

later the patrol returned to report that the bridge had collapsed into the canal and *Eisen* was holding its position against determined Belgian resistance. As a result of ground fog that partially obscured the objective the *Eisen* gliders had landed more dispersed than the other three assault groups. Fire from the *2e Grenadiers* set one of the gliders on fire on its landing approach although the occupants managed to scramble out after the aircraft touched down. *Leutnant* Schaechter was wounded not long after landing and *Leutnant* Joachim Meissner assumed command. Reinforced by the machine gun teams the *Fallschirmjäger* beat off three counterattacks mounted by the *2e Grenadiers*. In their drive to link up with Witzig's force at Eben-Emael the leading elements of IR 151 reached the eastern side of the canal at about 16.00 but it was the following morning before the regiment formally relieved Meissner. *Sturmgruppe Eisen* withdrew to Maastricht having suffered the heaviest casualties of the four assault groups - 22 dead, 26 wounded and one missing.

Able to cross the intact bridges at Vroenhoven and Veltwezelt the *4.Panzer-Division* quickly threatened to outflank the *2e Grenadiers* and the regiment was ordered on the evening of 11 May to withdraw to Liège along with the rest of the division before it was completely surrounded. The *2e Grenadiers* lost 10 officers and 207 other ranks killed, about 50 wounded and 190 taken prisoner in the fighting around Kanne and in recognition of its sacrifice the regiment was later awarded the battle honour 'Channel Albert – Kanne'.

Only 14 hours after the start of the offensive in the West the German Army had breached the Albert Canal and shattered General Gamelin's hope that the Belgian Army would be able to hold their forward defensive line for five days.

ALLIED REACTION

Less than three hours after the start of the German invasion General Gamelin, convinced that the enemy's main thrust into France would be through the Low Countries, ordered the implementation of his 'Plan D'. On the

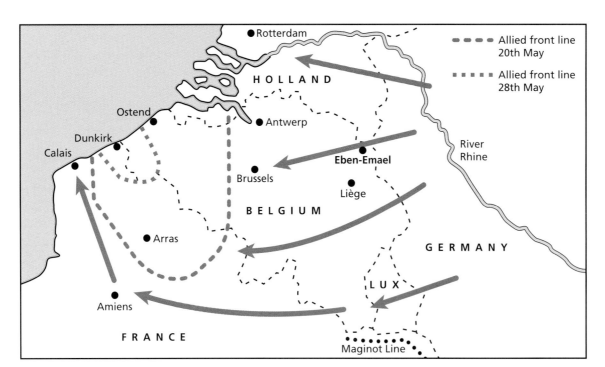

evening of the 10 May the French *Groupe d'Armée 1* (1 Army Group), including the *1re Armée* (1st Army) and the British Expeditionary Force, began moving toward the Breda-Dyle line. Hitler later said that when he learned the news: 'I could have wept for joy; they'd fallen into my trap!' Facing little opposition on its move through the Ardennes the leading formations of Germany's Army Group A reached the River Meuse late on 12 May and to the shock of the Allied high command the Germans successfully crossed the river the following day. Caught off balance the Allies rapidly collapsed. The Netherlands surrendered on 15 May, the first tanks of Army Group A reached the Channel coast on 20 May, the evacuation of the BEF from Dunkirk began on 26 May and the following day Belgium surrendered. The efforts of the new French Supreme Commander General Maxime Weygand to conduct a defence in depth were too late and on 22 June the French government signed an armistice with Germany.

LIÈGE FORTS

As Belgian field forces withdrew from Liège before the advance of Army Group B the forts of PFL I and PFL II were left isolated. Nevertheless, the three remaining PFL I forts continued to resist, providing fire support to each other to beat off infantry attacks.

Right: **Hitler addressing the** *Fallschirmjäger* **troops from the raid on Eben-Emael.** *(BA)*

Below: **The same ceremony of the presentation of Iron Cross decorations to the** *Fallschirmjäger.* **From the opposite direction the photographer for this view is in the centre of the rear group in the above picture.** *(JSS)*

The Germans used a combination of Ju87s and artillery to systematically reduce the Belgian emplacements. The flat trajectory of armour-piercing shells fired from 88mm guns proved effective in picking off observation cupolas. The *Hohlladungwaffe,* deployed by regular sappers, was also used against the fort. The defenders of Aubin-Neufchâteau surrendered on 21 May after their last gun emplacement was knocked out and by which time their ammunition was virtually exhausted. For a loss of six killed the defenders inflicted more than 2,000 casualties upon the Germans. Battice surrendered the next day after its last heavy gun became inoperable. As Fort Tancremont was situated in rougher terrain than its companion forts the defenders had time to complete their demolition and obstacle plan before the Germans attacked. The fort did not surrender until 29 May, the day after the Belgian Army was ordered to lay down its arms.

MEDALS ALL ROUND

On 16 May Hitler presented the *Ritterkreuz* (Knight's Cross of the Iron Cross) to the officers of *Sturmabteilung Koch,* with the exception of those wounded, at his forward headquarters, *Führerhauptquartier* Felsennest. Six days later he presented the same decoration to *Oberstleutnant* Mikosch and *Oberfeldwebel* Portsteffen.

Many of the soldiers at Eben-Emael bravely manned the emplacements until the fort surrendered. The garrisons of the other PFL I also fought as long as they could.

6

CONCLUSION

The *Wehrmacht's* daily report for 11 May proclaimed that 'the strongest fort of the Liège fortifications, Eben-Emael, had surrendered this Saturday afternoon. The commander and 1,000 men were taken prisoner. The fort had been incapacitated early on 10 May by a group selected from the *Luftwaffe* under *Oberleutnant* Witzig who had adopted new methods of attack.'

In his after action report Witzig described three reasons for the success of his mission:

- 'The shattered morale of the garrison, linked to the fear that we were already inside the casemates.'
- 'The weakening of the fortress defences caused by the loss of a number of the defensive posts, and the apparent uncertainty attached to which posts had been lost and whether the outer defences were holding.'
- 'The lack of support – other than of indirect artillery support – and of reinforcement from outside. Because of this it was not possible to mount a strong counterattack. 40 infantrymen were sent in to counterattack; of these only 12 survived.'

Left: **Officers of the German occupying force examine** *Coupole 120. (JSS)*

Right: **Lanaye bridge viewed from captured positions at *Bloc 01* to the south of Eben-Emael. German army engineers have just begun to assemble a pontoon bridge. This photograph is dated May 1940.** *(JSS)*

These reasons partially explain the Belgian failures at Eben-Emael rather than the many factors that contributed to the stunning German success.

Sturmabteilung Koch was a cohesive fighting force built on the foundation of a demanding selection process and tough parachute training and completed by realistic mission training in its teams. Alefts of *7 Trupp* said of his comrades in a post war interview: 'There was unyielding determination in each man's eyes. Those who are our friends, are our strong loyal friends; those who are our enemies will find us unyielding enemies. With this feeling we could search out the devil in hell!' The men of *Sturmabteilung Koch* knew they were the first of new breed of warriors bringing innovative tactics and weapons to the battlefield.

Whereas the German *Fallschirmjäger* rightly considered themselves to be members of an elite fighting group Eben-Emael's defenders were a disparate mix of professional soldiers, conscripts and reservists. Despite the vast expense of building Eben-Emael there was no prestige associated with a posting to a fortress regiment. Indeed, many of the garrison were

Right: **Lanaye bridge. The pontoon bridge is now complete but German infantry and artillery have crossed the canal by a route over a bridge which was captured intact.** *(JSS)*

Above:
Maastricht 2 after vegetation, covering it for many years has been removed. *(FE-E)*

Left: The damage inside Mi-Sud from a single 50kg *Hohlladungwaffe* placed by *9 Trupp*. *(FE-E)*

Above: Bloc II was not put out of action by Fallschirmjäger on 10 May 1940. It was attacked by Pionierbataillon 51 (Pioneer Battalion 51), commanded by Oberfeldwebel Josef Portsteffen, using Flammenwerfer 35 (flamethrower 35) and then a 50kg Hohlladungwaffe. (FE-E)

either unfit for field service or posted to the fort to be near their families or an important civilian job. Morale was poor and Jottrand's solution was to grant leave even though it reduced the garrison and did nothing to build unit esprit. The Belgian Army of 9 May 1940, that of a neutral country still at peace, was in a reactive mode. Many of the soldiers at Eben-Emael bravely manned their emplacements until the fort surrendered and the garrisons of the other PFL I also fought as long as they could. The 'fortress mentality' inherent in manning permanent fortifications did not build a spirit of aggression. The overly complex command structure imposed upon Jottrand did nothing to encourage rapid decision making. Complacency seemed to characterise the reaction to the alarm from Liège in the early hours of 10 May. Jottrand's hesitation about raising the barracks was a major reason that many of the fort's defenders were not at their posts. Three earlier alarms had passed without the need to destroy the barracks. Jottrand and many other Belgian commanders believed that morning that the situation would become clearer over time and they would have time to

react. However, the use of the glider robbed him of that time. Nevertheless, Jottrand succeeded in blowing the Kanne bridge and but for a few minutes, or a locked door, the defenders at Vroenhoven might have also destroyed that bridge.

As an integral part of the *Luftwaffe* Germany's airborne forces enjoyed a unity of command that was unique in World War Two. A single, clear chain of command directed every aspect of *Sturmabteilung Koch's* mission on 10 May. Göring, Kesselring, Student and other *Luftwaffe* officers were determined the operation would succeed, in spite of scepticism from some senior army officers, and ensured that Koch did not lack in resources.

The German military command philosophy of *Auftragstaktik* (mission-oriented command) was exemplified by the assault on Eben-Emael. *Auftragstaktik* is a decentralised leadership and command style that requires leaders at the lowest level to act on their own initiative to ensure that a mission is achieved. Junior leaders require a thorough understanding of their commander's intention at the beginning of an operation so that they can work toward

Above: **A close-up view of *Mi-Nord* and the damage from a 50kg hollow-charge weapon.** *(FE-E)*

it without requiring constant direction from their superiors. Not only the non-commissioned officers but also the individual soldiers of *Sturmabteilung Koch* were thoroughly briefed on the mission of their squads and platoons. Extensive and realistic rehearsals ensured that all ranks knew the plan and were prepared to cope with situations such as the loss of a glider or a team leader. The nine squads that landed on Eben-Emael completed their first assignments without being aware that their platoon commander had not arrived on the objective. *Hauptfeldwebel* Wenzel stressed that 'the officers had trained all of the men so well that the officers were expendable'. Well trained, aggressive soldiers such as Wenzel at Eben-Emael, and *Leutnant* Meissner at Kanne bridge, took charge without hesitation. The determination of *Leutnant* Witzig and *Oberjäger* Meier to reach *Sturmgruppe Granit* are clear examples of the initial initiative that is the basis of *Auftragstaktik*.

When Hitler briefed Student on his concept to seize Eben-Emael by *coup de main* he stressed the need for secrecy if the audacious plan was to succeed. This emphasis on security throughout the command structure enabled the Germans to achieve strategic surprise with the timing of their offensive, operational surprise by first luring the Allies into Belgium and then striking through the Ardennes, and tactical surprise at Eben-Emael and the Albert Canal bridges.

Tactical surprise, the key to the entire operation, would not have been possible without the use of the DFS 230 glider which enabled *Sturmabteilung Koch* to attack silently from the one direction – above – that the Belgians had not anticipated and for which they were least prepared. Careful selection and training ensured that the glider pilots, particularly those of Witzig's group, exploited the DFS 230's excellent handling characteristics and landed their teams within tens of metres of their objectives. Landing as complete squads with their weapons and demolitions equipment the *Fallschirmjäger* were able to attack without hesitation. This sudden, violent assault gave the Germans the initiative from the start of

Above: Mi-Sud was to have been the objective of 2 Trupp and the alternate for 11 and 3 Trupp. After years of being covered in vegetation it was cleared in 2005 by volunteers to reveal Mi-Sud in almost 'new' condition complete with armoured observation cupola. (FE-E)

the battle. The use of the DFS230 achieved precisely what Hitler had hoped.

The *Hohlladungwaffe*, the second technical innovation employed at Eben-Emael, did not achieve the full 'Neumann Effect' because of its inefficient design. The fort's emplacements were neutralised by a combination of repeated *Hohlladungwaffe* attacks and conventional demolition charges. However, the violent *Hohlladungwaffe* blasts had a psychological effect on the Belgian garrison that should not be underestimated. It is understandable that the defenders, isolated in their casemates and cupolas, believed that the small numbers of enemy attacking them were using some kind of secret weapon. Many were undoubtedly relieved when they realised the Germans were not using poison gas. Although the gliders were quickly removed from Eben-Emael it was the use of the *Hohlladungwaffe* that the Germans were most concerned about keeping under wraps. Under a direct order from Hitler the penetrations caused by the *Hohlladungwaffe* were filled with concrete before foreign military attaches were allowed to inspect Eben-Emael. The allies were mystified

as to how a fort regarded as one of the strongest and most modern in the world had been captured so quickly. Göbbels compounded this uncertainty when he talked of a 'new method of warfare' that many observers believed to be a veiled reference to poison gas. The fall of Eben-Emael may have undermined French confidence in the Maginot Line but the German breakthrough in the Ardennes, indeed German's new method of warfare, quickly made France's vaunted fortifications irrelevant.

Sturmabteilung Koch undertook one of the most audacious operations of the World War Two that fully exploited new technology to maximum effect. After the war General Student said: 'It was a deed of exemplary daring and decisive significance. A handful of paratroops, with powerful support by the air force, forced a passage for an army to break through. I have studied the history of the last war and the battles on all fronts. But I have not been able to find anything among the host of brilliant actions – undertaken by friend or foe – that could be said to compare with the success achieved by Koch's assault group.'

Above: Reichsmarschall Hermann Göring meets *Fallschirmjäger*. The troops are wearing standard parachute equipment, but the photograph is from later than Eben-Emael as the legged-jacket worn is of the camouflage pattern. *(JSS)*